Memories of
Crewe & Nantwich

The publishers would like to thank the following companies for their support in the production of this book

Barratt's Coaches

British Salt

Flowcrete

Jaymar Packaging

Malbank School & Sixth Form College

F J Need

Nantwich Funeral Services

Poole Alcock LLP

Reaseheath College

Speakman & Co.

First published in Great Britain by True North Books Limited
England HX3 6SN
01422 244555
www.truenorthbooks.com

ISBN 978 - 1906649647

Text, design and origination by True North Books
Printed and bound by The Charlesworth Group

Memories of Crewe & Nantwich

CONTENTS

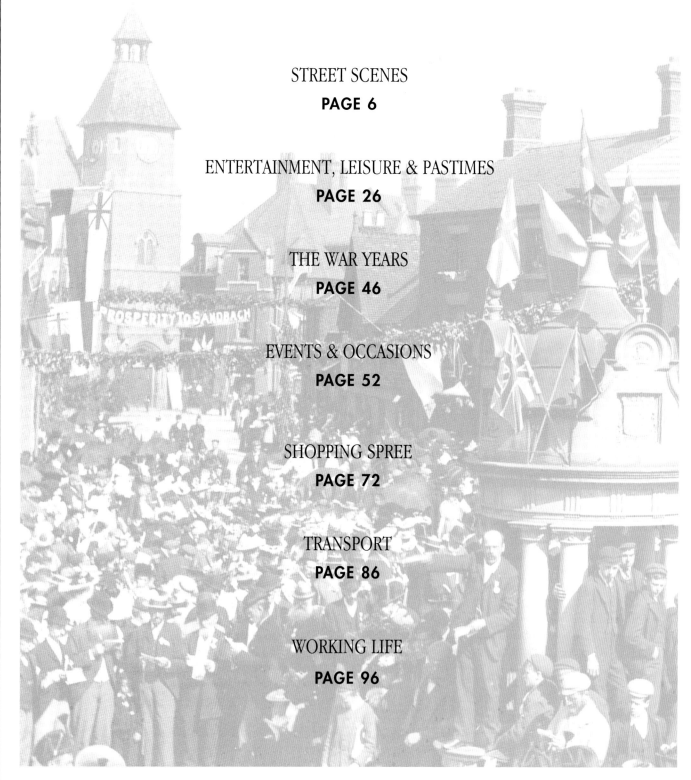

INTRODUCTION

You are about to enjoy a voyage of discovery into times gone by, brought to you by 'Crewe and Nantwich Memories'. As the reader turns the pages, a visit is made to those days of up to a century ago when the pace of life was so different, the sights and sounds of our towns so far removed from those of today and the standards to which we adhered were so dissimilar. Buildings have changed, streets have disappeared and styles altered dramatically. The way in which we dressed, the manner in which we moved around and the sources of our entertainment seem, in many ways, alien to those who are only aware of the culture of today's environment. Yet, without all that went before, there would not be a present. But for the horse drawn tram there would be no bus, but for Henry Hall there would be no Take That and but for the corner shop no Market Centre. Only by looking back at the times through which our parents and grandparents lived can we begin to make sense of what we have now.

This book makes no apologies for helping unleash waves of nostalgia in the psyche of readers who recognise the places captured by the photographs inside these covers. This is all part of reliving the past as you are invited to join in that rolling back of time. Once again, you will be able to see the gaslamps above the shop facades on Victoria Street, hear the clank of the tramcars bowling along Earle Street and pop into the newsagents on High Street to get a copy of the Daily Herald along with the latest issue of Film Fun. Thanks to the contents of this book you can imagine chewing some gum and puffing away on a Camel, given to you by one of those wartime GIs with a seemingly endless supply of money. You will be able to remember your own childhood or be reminded of that of your forebears when reading the captions or viewing the lovely photographs. Playing hide and seek in Queen's Park, making a den on the spare land at the end of the lane or games of tig and rally-o on the cobbled streets are part of our heritage. Will our great-grandchildren really come, in time, to regard the Playstation and Nintendo DS as the equivalent of the spinning top, yoyo and hula-hoop? Perhaps they will.

'Crewe and Nantwich Memories' is not a definitive and dusty old tome that is just another history book. It is aimed at stimulating the nostalgia cells within the mind, if there are any such bits of our brain that can be so described. Without the content of this book and others of its genre, much of what we had would be lost forever. Thankfully, we can also look back at the old industries that helped make this part of Cheshire such a special place in which to live. Crewe, of course, is a comparatively modern town. It was not formally laid out until the middle of the 19th century and relied heavily upon the railways for its very being. Though considerably smaller, Nantwich has strong links with salt working and can trace its roots back to at least Roman times. The town even boasts over 100 listed buildings on its streets. Not everything is viewed through rose tinted lenses. There is also a sense of realism in the book as darker times are acknowledged. There were the two major wars of the last century, the depression days of the 1930s and the poverty and low life expectancy experienced by the working classes in their ill-appointed properties of the early 20th century. 'Crewe and Nantwich Memories' does not ignore these as they belong to the building blocks that made us the Cheshire folk we are today.

The companies and organisations which have developed and thrived in the town over recent decades are many. We take pleasure in including in this book histories of an outstanding selection of different companies whose contribution to the development and sustainability of the town's economic prosperity is a matter of record. With their co-operation and access to their respective photographic archives, we have been able to tell their stories and hopefully trigger the memories of local people who have worked for them or been touched by their part in community life. Perhaps now is a good time to start to turn the first page and enter into the time that grandpa told us about when we were on his knee. Stick a Spangle into your mouth and pour a glass of milk stout, just like Ena Sharples used to enjoy in the snug of her local. Wind up the gramophone and put on a scratchy rendition of 'Tico Tico' by those gorgeous Andrews Sisters. Join some old friends in these pages who still think that grass is for walking on and not for smoking and that 'please' and 'thank you' are still part of our vocabulary. Renew acquaintance with a housewife rather than a working mother and take your seat on the bus that a young child has given up for you. Now, there's a memory.

TEXT	ANDREW MITCHELL
PHOTOGRAPH RESEARCH	TONY LAX
DESIGNER	SEAMUS MOLLOY
BUSINESS DEVELOPMENT EDITOR	PETER PREST

STREET SCENES

Coppenhall Terrace was home to the old statutory market that was established by the Local Board in 1848. It was then a cheese and cattle market and this part of town eventually became known as Market Square. In the early part of the last century, Coppenhall Terrace was a popular spot for apprentices and their potential belles to take a Sunday stroll. They walked back and forth from the Square to the General Offices. Couples referred to this as 'taking a walk round the Green', meaning Crewe Green, and continuing on past the station. Of course, the Sabbath was a day of rest, not just another shopping opportunity with free parking to attract the crowds as it has now become. Retail is the new religion, it would seem, as we worship at the altar of the cut price bargain. It was a more considered and orderly affair along this terrace in 1919. The paper boy standing in the middle of the road carried news that was to shape the future of Europe for years to come. We had just emerged from that horrendous four-year war that left millions dead and as many again maimed and traumatised. The Treaty of Versailles was drawn up and, with Lloyd George promising 'to squeeze Germany like a lemon until the pips squeak', lands were taken from the vanquished in an act of both reparation and revenge. The Germans festered under what they viewed as an injustice and this helped provide the breeding ground for the eventual rise to power of a certain little Austrian born ex-corporal with a funny moustache.

Above: Farmers' markets have made something of a comeback in recent years. They are especially popular in Nantwich and the last Saturday in every month is an experience not to be missed. The streets and stalls are alive with action and entertainment in addition to the sale of goods and produce that we all expect. It was just as lively an affair back in 1900. Market Day was an important occasion and the town centre and neighbouring streets packed with horse drawn carts and wagons piled high with fresh fruit, vegetables, poultry, game, dairy products and other foodstuffs that had been brought in from the neighbouring farms and smallholdings. Elsewhere, pots, pans and other implements were on sale, along with wools, yarns and clothing that were laid out for housewives to check for quality and value for money. Street entertainers came along to try to earn a few shillings with their juggling acts and feats of acrobatics. Occasionally, a fire-eater would display his prowess and travelling medicine men extolled the virtues of various patent remedies that they peddled. On the down side, the regular market was also a good place for pickpockets to use their skills and there were also times when men imbibed too well and not wisely enough. Some horses knew their way home without the need for a hand on the reins, which was just as well as the owner was sleeping it off in the back of the cart.

Right: The view along Crewe Road shows the main street in Wheelock leading towards the bridge, south of Sandbach, at a time in the early 1900s. The village name means 'winding river'. Lorry drivers were hammering along this road in the middle of the last century, but Wheelock returned to a more sedate environment when the A534 bypass was built.

Right: The infant in the pram outside 87 Station Road, Winsford, was in training for a role as James Bond in later life. In that boneshaker of a contraption he would have emerged after any length of journey shaken if not stirred! Sleep was not a commodity to be practised while out and about being pushed along the setts that guaranteed a bumpy ride. Note how well clad everyone was for this photograph taken around the turn into the 20th century. The woman at her front door has even donned a clean apron for the occasion. Note the gleaming front step that had probably been donkey stoned that morning. The boot scrapers either side of the door pillars made sure that hubby cleaned his footwear before entering the house. This was a woman who took pride in her appearance and that of her home. Station Road connected with the waterfront of the River Weaver, making it a useful transport link for barges and railway wagons. The Winsford Lodge, a three star guest house, now occupies the site where 85 and 87 Station Road provided family accommodation. The terraced housing has long been consigned to history. Gardens and open land can now be found among a mixture of older and more modern semis that are popular in this locality today.

Above: Pillory Street in Nantwich takes its obvious name from the form of punishment once used here. The old pillory still stands to the left of where the photographer took up his position over 100 years ago as he aimed his lens at and beyond the temperance hotel and towards High Street. This large building on the right, built in 1897, is now home to Intimo Design. It was formerly the Victorian Cocoa House and opened as a non-alcoholic oasis within the plethora of public houses, inns and beerhouses that populated Nantwich in those days. Close by, the small shopping area that is Cocoa Yard keeps a named link with when Victorians tried to counter the evils of demon drink. The Players' Theatre is situated behind the pillory, in between a pair of fast-food shops and across the road from Nantwich Museum, founded in 1980 in the former library building that itself was sited where the gaol used to be. That latter place was for more wicked folk than those who found themselves pilloried. The pillory was a device made of a wooden or metal framework erected on a post, with holes for securing the head and hands. It was similar to the stocks, but the latter had holes for securing the feet and, sometimes, the hands as well. Whatever the arrangement, both contraptions were designed to punish people by means of public humiliation. They could be mocked or have rubbish thrown at them. Incarceration in the pillory was more dangerous than in the stocks as the victim had to stand with his head largely immobilised. Further punishments could also be administered on them, such as caning or whipping. The pillory was abolished in 1837 and the stocks not used after 1872. Some think that they would make a good alternative to the 21st century ASBO.

Below: Welsh Row is the start of the road out to Chester from the town centre, beginning where it crosses the River Weaver. These buildings, viewed from close to a spot that is now home to the furniture shop, Mia Stanza, are largely as they were at the start of the Edwardian era. The hotel on the right was known as the Three Pigeons. Situated at 20-22 Welsh Row, it is thought to have been built on the site of an even older establishment. Two 'salt ships', namely brine barrels, were discovered buried here. Now a Grade II listed building, it had a long career as a well known and popular, traditional inn. In recent years it was turned into a restaurant, bar and nightclub, called the Nakatcha. The buildings to the left at 26-30 are also listed and for a time were known as Carshaw's bar. More recently, called the Cheshire Cat, a new concept venue for eating, drinking and napping. They began life in 1637 as cottages and were converted to three almshouses, housing six widows, in 1676 by Sir Roger Wilbraham. The death of his wife and children moved him to help provide for the more needy. A worn stone mounting block, with several steps up to the top from where a huntsman might have mounted his steed, adorns the front of this piece of history. The almshouses have been preserved for us largely thanks to the work of William Schofield (1903-85). Saddened by the sight of the largely derelict buildings at the end of the last war, he vowed to prevent further deterioration and to restore them to something of their former glory. He spent six years on his labour of love. To the left of here, there is now a set of office buildings, with a beauty salon beyond. To the right, by the oldest gateway into Nantwich, today we can find Clough's paint and wallpaper shop.

Below: In the 1960s Tesco opened Crewe's first supermarket in the area to the right, on a site that in more recent times belonged to Ethel Austin, the children's wear retail outlet. The view down Earle Street, from Market Street, takes us past the old Adelphi Hotel on the left and the Market Hall. This latter building dates from 1854 and was purchased by the Council in 1869. Beyond there lie the Municipal Buildings, built in 1905 by architect Henry T Hare. Formerly home to Crewe and Nantwich Borough Council, they are now run by Cheshire East Council. The buildings to the right have been cleared and the war memorial, moved from Market Square in 2006, now looks out across this space. The route towards Stoke-on-Trent, over the railway bridge, was littered with horse droppings in 1910. The sight of a motor car was still something of a novelty and the four legged friend remained a major source of power for wheeled transport and conveyances. Naturally, gardeners and those with a liking for rhubarb appeared at regular intervals with buckets and shovels. Even so, there was still an odour and a host of flies that did not make highways pleasant places upon which to linger for too long.

Above: The A5019, Mill Street, runs north from the A534 towards the roundabout at Vernon Way. There is little evidence today of the late Victorian buildings that provided homes for the Crewe working classes of the time as the street is now a mixture of open spaces, car parking areas, industrial units and shops, with only a small proportion of Mill Street now being classed as residential. Although people had become used to having their picture taken in studio portraits and at weddings and similar functions, a photographer out and about on the town's roads was something of a novelty. This cameraman attracted a number of inquisitive bystanders who were happy to be snapped for what would turn out to be a historical view of a place close to the centre of Crewe and its railway heartland.

soon to be found on virtually every High Street in the land. The droppings on the cobblestones outside its door tell us that the horse was a common beast of burden and source of pulling power back then. The bicycle was a popular alternative way of getting about and we can see several examples of pedal propulsion heading across The Square. It was still something of a boneshaker ride

Above right: Nantwich has a connection with WH Smith that dates back over a century. The internationally famous bookseller has two current outlets on the edge of Nantwich Square. The one on the left was pictured at the turn into the 20th century. It is perhaps appropriate that WH Smith has had such a long link with the town. It has a lengthy history of its own. Henry Smith founded a London based news vendor business in the late 18th century and, after his death, his younger son, William Henry, took it over, renaming it as WH Smith and Son in 1845. The company expanded to include printing facilities and the name was

as the cobbled setts of the highway were not conducive to comfort. Even so, two wheels were better and quicker than two feet for getting around. It was Dunlop's invention of the pneumatic tyre in 1888 that heralded a golden age for cycling in late Victorian and early Edwardian times. The pushbike became a source of practical transport and a major leisure pursuit as well. Now, the horse manure may have gone, but much of this vista is still recognisable. Nantwich is second only to Chester as a mainstay of Cheshire heritage in the number of listed buildings that it supports.

The photographer stood on the pavement at the crossroads with Chester Street, looking along Market Street towards Crewe's Market Square. The bobby on the right was probably heading off to the police station on Edleston Road. Things were quieter on our streets in 1927 and the police did not have to walk around in pairs as they do in our town centres today. Where the trees on the left once stood, we now have the NatWest bank building. The handsome edifice on the corner on the right does business as a bookmaker's and finance certainly seems to dominate this part of town. The other shops on that side have given way to the Nationwide Building Society, HSBC Bank and a cheque cashing, money lending outlet.

Above: You would now be looking at the roundabout on Vernon Way as the eye follows Earle Street out towards the railway bridge. There was no need for such traffic flow aids in the 1920s and pedestrians as well as cars and carts happily shared the highway. The road was dominated by the grand Market Hall and Municipal Buildings, just as this side of the street is today. The other buildings remain, with a jeweller later on the far side of Hill Street where the Oxo poster had been pasted. RL Kilner's shop was latterly Time Tunnel and the Cheese Hall Hotel became The Three Lamps, retaining a tenuous connection with the standard we can see on the corner of the pub. However, by late 2010 the old name for this hotel was resurrected, reminding locals and visitors alike of the commodity that was traded in these quarters in earlier times. With the nearby Lyceum Square redevelopment coming to fruition, this part of Crewe began to take on a new look as the second decade of this century got under way. The Lyceum Theatre provides the centre piece to that top end of Hill Street. Built in 1911 and refurbished in 1994, the theatre kept its delightful auditorium with exquisite carvings, stalls, circle, upper gallery and wonderfully gilded private boxes.

Bottom left: Although the motor car and lorry had long been seen on our town and city streets, Britain still retained links with its gentler and more rural past, even as late as the inter-war years. Even though it was 1928, the Market Square in Crewe had room for the horse and cart making a delivery of milk churns. Marks & Spencer now trades from this position on the right. The far side of the square was known as Market Terrace and now belongs to Queensway. The gentlemen discussing the current news were somewhat heated in their opinions. It seemed that all women over the age of 21 were now entitled to vote. It had been something of a shock when the government gave in to those noisy, demented suffragettes and let females into the voting booths nearly a decade earlier, but at least they were adults of 30 and more. To grant, what were little more than girls, parity with men was a bit rich, to say the least. The men also grumbled about the state of female fashion. Young women were cropping their hair short, wearing coloured stockings and displaying their knees as hemlines inched ever higher. Not all oldtimers were such fuddy-duddies. The writer, George Bernard Shaw, described the feminine look as 'fit for real human beings rather than upholstery for Victorian angels'.

Below: Although we talk of the 1920s as either being a roaring decade or one that ushered in the years of the Depression, for many it was just another series of days, weeks and months. Many people were not touched by the flappers dancing the Black Bottom or the despair of those on Wall Street as their holdings in various companies became worthless. The elderly couple and their companion cared little for all of that. They were happy to take the air under the leafy boughs that made part of Coppenhall Terrace appear as if it were some sort of French boulevard. The chap puffing on his pipe listened to the conversation of the women with only half an ear. That is what men have done for hundreds of years and still do today. It does, of course, infuriate their companions, but a man's skin is as thick as his head, as many a wife has been known to comment. Coppenhall Terrace was an ideal spot for a meander along the road. It led away from the heart of town, but was still close enough for a pedestrian to feel that he was still close to the action, though our trio would not have used that sort of terminology in those days.

Right: These two images are taken on Boots Corner almost 40 years apart. In the first picture from 1920, it is unlikely the two policemen in shot are discussing the price of cosmetics. They could however be talking about the fact that Boots had just been sold to the American United Drug Company. However, deteriorating economic circumstances in North America saw Boots sold back into British hands in 1933.

Below: The women waiting outside Boots wore typically flounced skirts over petticoats that symbolised female fashion in the late 1950s. They were very impressive as they flared out on a Saturday night when a girl showed off her prowess in the jive at the local dance hall. The fellow on the left had his own sense of fashion with his bicycle clips firmly clamping his trousers legs to his ankles. The younger man heading right was quite a dapper chappie in his cravat. The Boots shop is one of those British institutions that we would feel lost without should it ever disappear from our town centres. Jesse Boot, later ennobled as Lord Trent, transformed the company founded in 1849 by his father into that of a national retailer. The Boot family

lived in a poor part of Nottingham and Jesse's father opened a small shop in the town selling herbal remedies. After his father's death, a very young Jesse went into partnership with his mother. As business boomed, more outlets were opened outside Nottingham in the latter part of the 19th century. In the early 1900s, Boot's started to buy out other chemists and open further shops until the company was established nationwide. By 1933, two years after Jesse died, the 1,000th Boots opened in Galashiels. By then, he was known as a benefactor, having contributed substantially to many worthy causes.

Above: This was Victoria Street as it appeared in 1938, with the car heading towards the camera away from Market Street. Although World War II was only a short period of time away, the people of Crewe went about their business largely unaware of the devastation that was to

follow. In the meantime, life went on as best it could. The buses carried their passengers to and from town. Crosville was the main company we saw on our roads at the time. It was founded in 1906 in Chester by George Crosland Taylor and Georges de Ville. They intended to go into business manufacturing motor cars, but soon diversified into public transport when they ran a service with their own buses between Chester and Ellesmere Port in 1909. The car making side of the company only lasted until 1908. Crosville was the most prominent name on our county's buses for over half a century. The formation of the National Bus Company in 1968, followed by further legislation in 1986, caused the Crosville influence to be weakened. Over the next few years it was fragmented to such a degree that only three depots were left under its control by the late 1980s. Even the company name disappeared in 1990 when it was rebranded as North British Bus Ltd.

Above: A veritable host of traffic made its way up Crewe's High Street from Edleston Road in 1938, leaving behind the Plaza Cinema and Kettell's Hotel on the left. This part of town is now somewhat run down, with its host of fast food shops and Asian eating places. The taller building on the left, outside which the lady cyclist has paused, is currently a snooker hall. The centrally strung street lamps are delightful period pieces and the Belisha beacon similarly so. The silver studs in the highway, indicating the track a pedestrian should follow, did not become the standard zebra markings we now associate with such a crossing until the very early 1950s. The beacon was named for the Minister of Transport who oversaw a raft of safety measures being introduced on our roads in the 1930s. We had a shocking road safety record compared with the rest of Europe. This gives the lie to tales about mad Italians and loony French drivers. They were far more responsible than we were and the measures that their governments took to protect road users from others and themselves were more advanced than anything we did. It was not until the start of this decade that electrically operated traffic lights appeared in any number on our road junctions and crossroads. Percy Shaw did not start to manufacture his reflective cat's eyes until the mid 1930s and it was only really during the blackout after 1939 that the country fully realised their benefits. The Highway Code, giving advice to drivers in particular, came along in 1931, but a driving test for those new behind the wheel took another four years to get organised on a compulsory basis. Leslie Hore-Belisha became the responsible Minister in 1934. One of his first moves was to reintroduce the 30 mph speed limit in built-up areas. Amazingly, this had been removed in 1930, leading to a speeding free for all. The pedestrian crossing and beacon that share his name were major moves in giving those on foot greater protection. The general public chose to call it after him. By the time of this photograph, Hore-Belisha had been moved to the War Ministry, where he was to stay until 1940. After retiring from politics in the 1950s, he was an appropriate choice as the vice president of the Pedestrians' Association.

This page: There are many similarities in these two photographs from Market Square, just over 10 years apart. The war memorial held pride of place in the centre. This statue was placed to commemorate the men of Crewe who seeking the welfare of their country gave their lives in so doing and are now resting in and beyond the seas. To the right, Marks & Spencer was the main store we can see, just as it is these days. The Odeon seen on the left was still popular in the 1950s, however, cinema-going in general was beginning a decline. Audience numbers began to fall off drastically for a variety of reasons. Improved housing and affordable television sets were reducing the incentive to go out for entertainment. Hollywood was no longer making so many of the escapist family entertainment films. A large number of UK cinemas closed in the 1960s. Those that struggled through this period of decline underwent twinning or tripling to reduce auditorium size and increase choice. But by the mid-1980s cinema attendance was at an all time low.... the Odeon in Crewe closed in 1983. Apart from the ornate lampost, the obvious difference between the two images is the erection of the clock tower on Queensway. The tower was built in 1957 and has dominated the skyline around the Marketplace ever since. The image below is from the mid 1960s and this busy part of town was experiencing something of a boom. We will leave you to decide whether modern is better.

Above: The lorry driver about to turn onto Exchange Street needed to take care coming across the traffic. However, the volume of motor vehicles on our roads was so much smaller half a century ago. In 1960, you could still find somewhere to park at the kerbside, even near a town centre. There were always plenty of gaps in the traffic, so queuing at junctions was not the hassle that it would become. More built-up areas had begun to suffer from traffic jams by 1960 as car ownership began to increase. By the end of the decade, things had changed dramatically. Most families had their own vehicles. The car became something of a necessity and not the luxury it had been either side of the war. At the time of the photograph, all that mattered little to the man on the left in his overalls and the woman in front, handbag firmly clasped. They would be availing themselves of public transport for some time yet.

Left: In July 1962, it was perfectly all right for ladies to have a chinwag on Delamere Street as they took a short break from their shopping. After all, you just have to catch up on the gossip when you bump into an old friend whom you may not have seen for at least two days. The world could have changed dramatically during that period. Never mind that Prime Minister Macmillan was sacking half his Cabinet or that the world's first passenger hovercraft had just crossed the Dee estuary, these women wanted to know the latest about Mrs Backhouse's wayward daughter and Mrs Ramsbottom's stay-away husband. Our chattering ladies on the right were housewives. These were the roles that were something to which most women aspired. Marry your man, get settled in a house and have a few children and you were set for life. The younger generation of mums, seen with their prams outside the old Post Office, would be the last with this sort of attitude. As they waited to collect their Family Allowance, the swinging 60s were under way. By the end of the decade, women's lib would be on the agenda, with the following decade witnessing bras on bonfires. The unwieldy term 'Ms' would do away with the need to differentiate between Miss and Mrs, whether the person in question minded or not. The Odeon stood to the right and, when going to the cinema was a popular way of doing a bit of courting, the Post Office was a popular meeting place for couples from out of town before heading for the back row. In those days, the lad paid for his lass, but the feminists would have none of that in more modern times. Pragmatic males thought, 'Suit yourself', and pocketed their money, but romantics longed for the times when a man looked after his woman both financially and physically. Some women still did, but they dare not tell Ms Greer and her cronies.

Above: Looking along High Street, in Winsford, we are gazing towards the River Weaver. In the 1960s, people still wanted to get their 'divi' from the Co-op. They collected stamps that were generated by purchasing goods in the shop and, when the stamps filled a card, this could be exchanged for cash that would be then spent on further items. The chain was then started all over again. It became the oldest shopping bonus scheme in the world. It was scrapped in the 1970s, because of high administration costs and a little bit of history and tradition went as well.

Right: This aerial photograph was taken on 13 June, 1988. The view looks across the River Weaver and Water Lode from the southwest. Known as 'the cathedral of South Cheshire', St Mary's Church, dating from the 14th century, can be seen just to the right of centre of the scene. On the last Saturday in the month except December when the market is the Saturday before Christmas. The markets, streets and shops in this vicinity come to life in a truly vibrant fashion. Vendors, buskers, shoppers and visitors give the lovely old town a real buzz that sets it apart from many other places of a similar size. To the left hand side is the Oat Market, leading on to Beam Street, which then passes the current Nantwich bus station. Running away from the Parish Church to the right is London Road and Crewe Road.

Below: The Parish Church of St. Mary, Nantwich is a Grade 1 listed building, acknowledged to be one of the finest medieval town churches. Mostly 14th century construction, although a number of changes have since been made, particularly a substantial 19th century restoration by Sir George Gilbert Scott. The church and its fine octagonal tower are built in red sandstone and is a feature for miles around. Today it is a major tourist attraction with estimated visitors totalling 50,000 per year.

ENTERTAINMENT LEISURE & PASTIMES

It was sights such as this that inspired the Lancashire artist, LS Lowry, to paint his industrial scenes of matchstalk men, as in the 1930 work, 'Coming from the Mill'. The workers here were Crewe Locomotive Works employees, crossing Market Square in the 1880s. The smiles on the faces of those in the foreground suggest that their shift had just ended.

Above: There were probably two golden ages of cycling in Victorian times. The concept of two wheeled individual freedom began with the idea of Karl von Drais, a German who introduced a sort of walking bicycle that was a wheeled frame on which sat a rider who used his feet to propel his machine. Various French inventors added cranked pedals in the 1860s and this led to the production of Scotsman Thomas McCall's velocipede in 1869. Sussex pioneer, James Starley, developed a chain driven bicycle in the 1870s that progressed into the penny farthing cycle, as it later

became known. The first craze for two wheels began in earnest and soon our country lanes, highways and byways were hosting hordes of cyclists anxious to explore ever wider horizons than were available to them as mere pedestrians. The Crewe Wheelers, pictured c1880, was just one of many similar clubs formed for members to share an interest in exploration and competition. This was the start of the first golden age of cycling, followed by its successor a decade later after Mr Dunlop had invented his pneumatic tyre and the rear freewheel was developed, enabling the rider to coast. By the 1920s, there were five major cycling clubs in South Cheshire. Changes in recreational interests left the area with just two clubs in the 1960s and these amalgamated as the Crewe Clarion Wheelers in 1968. It currently has about 50 members.

Bottom left: As three generations of the same family, Mrs Rowley Lee, daughter Jean Joy and granddaughter May Joy, passed the Municipal Buildings on Earle Street, they would have been surprised to learn of the outcry that would greet two such

women today. Back in the 1920s, it was just fine and dandy to sport fox fur as a fashion accessory. Do it now and the Friends of this, that and the other would be upon you. In the 1950s, film starlets were given mink coats by old men with a twinkle in their eyes and society queens, such as Lady Docker, simply flaunted their sables in front of all and sundry. We had better stick with a Burberry wool cashmere today. Goat wool does not annoy the pc brigade, it seems.

Below: The children gathered happily in front of the war memorial not long after it had been erected in Queen's Park in memory of those who gave their lives in the Boer War. Crewe had a larger share of its population volunteering to serve in South Africa than any other town in the country. Unveiled on 8 August, 1903, it bears a distinctive life size figure of a soldier at its top and is guarded by lions at the base. A plate at the front carries a relief of a locomotive and tender. The copper bronze plaques on the four sides of the monument give the names of the railway volunteers who served in the conflict.

Below: After the last war, many of our towns and cities had large areas that had been flattened during German air raids. These bomb sites, as they were known, became car parks or impromptu children's playgrounds until they were built upon. Twenty years later, the same sort of situation repeated itself after councils began clearing areas under regeneration and redevelopment programmes. On a Sunday morning in February 1965, this group of children enjoyed the space on Havelock Street, created during the demolition process of the Mill Street area. With a hint of Enid Blyton's Famous Five, this Estimable Eight had its girl member. No doubt she could handle herself well enough and had earned the respect of her pals. These were days when children could actually play without having to plug something into the wall. Swinging off ropes on lampposts, scrambling over walls, kicking a ball down the street and playing rally-o, marbles, conkers and tig provided so much enjoyment. It was cheap entertainment and the sort of fun we provided for ourselves.

Top left and above: These two early images start a theme which is carried on over the years, and that is, improvisation was the name of the game. You didn't need a ball for football - a tightly bound bundle of rags or clothes would do. There were games that matched the seasons, conkers for example. Those determined to win used foul and dishonest ways to convert the simple conker into a hard and unyielding boulder to cheat their way to success. Later in the year, it was marbles with those wonderful glass beads put to aggressive and destructive use to determine who was top dog. There were also collecting activities, usually involving cards with familiar faces, often of footballers or film stars. Playground games were often determined by gender, with the differences usually marked by the polarising of physical prowess and single-mindedness on the one hand and a softer camaraderie and togetherness on the other. All the equipment and artefacts used in play were simple, often loud and often extremely irritating in their use and application, but great fun!

Right: The influence of Errol Flynn in the 1940s is obvious here in a game involving bows and arrows. His playing of Robin Hood against Olivia de Havilland as Maid Marian had a ground-breaking impact for some little boys that remained with them to their teenage years (and in some cases even longer!). Cinema has always had an influence on children's re-enactment and performance of stories and fables. Certainly, children in the 1940s rarely complained about boredom or having nothing to do. They simply grasped the nettle and worked out what they could turn it into and did it together.

Above: This is a very early picture of the Chetwode Arms which stood opposite St Paul's Church on the High Town crossroads, until it was controversially bulldozed in May, 1980, to make way for the West Street extension.

The 'Chetty' was a very popular public house in Crewe at the time and many locals still feel somewhat aggrieved that the pub had to be knocked down to accommodate the Traffic Alleviation scheme.

Below: The Bear's Head Hotel, now more of a motel with some modern additions and restyled as the Bear's Head Innkeeper's Lodge, was a meeting place for the Cheshire Hunt in the middle of the last century. Situated on Newcastle Road South, Brereton Green, near Sandbach, it looks little different from the one pictured here as riders and dogs prepared to take off as the 'unspeakable in pursuit of the uneatable', as Oscar Wilde neatly put it. The Cheshire Hunt was founded in 1763 and encompassed the entire county. This large area divided between the Cheshire and South Cheshire Hunts in 1877, before being reunited in 1907, separated again in 1931 and rejoined in 1946. The organisation continues to meet, despite the 2004 legislation and modern attitudes restricting its activities. Examples of urban foxes causing damage and even injury have made some question the wisdom of a blanket ban, but readers will have to make up their own minds about the best way in which to deal with Reynard. What cannot be denied is that the sight of a rider in hunting red, partaking of a stirrup cup on a frosty January morn, is somehow quintessentially English. Tally-ho.

Left: The Three Pigeons Homing Society met on 27 April, 1961, and members here are seen ringing a bird prior to its participation in a race. Pigeon racing requires a special breed of the species, known as the 'racing homer'. In the days of terraced housing and back yards, many men kept pigeons in small lofts they had lovingly built for their birds. Some spoke to them in more loving terms than those used to address their wives, though at least their spouses were allowed indoors! The sport is thought to be almost 2,000 years old and became particularly popular in Europe in the 19th century, thanks to a Belgian influence. Flemish migrant workers brought their interest to the countries to which they travelled and inspired others across the Continent to join in. The first official races in Britain took place in 1881. The Royal Family even got involved when King Leopold II of Belgium presented Queen Victoria with a breeding pair. In addition to racing competitions, homing pigeons have been used to carry messages by lovers conducting secret trysts and by the military, getting important, coded information to and from the front or passing information behind enemy lines. In case anyone finds the facts about wartime use too fanciful, then tell him to consult the list of Dickin Medal winners. Instituted in 1943 to honour the gallantry of animals in wartime, 26 medals were awarded between then and August 1945. Of these, 16 went to pigeons.

Below: Crewe Hall has a fascinating history, with it's origins dating back to 1170. It came into the Crewe family in 1608, but was in such a state of decay that it was demolished in 1615 and the rebuild completed in 1636. A fire broke out in the Hall in 1866 and the interior of the mansion was almost completely burnt out. The Hall had to be rebuilt again, and the third Baron of Crewe hired Edward Barry to supervise the work. Barry restored it with the wealth of mid-Victorian ornamentation that can be seen today. Over the years, Crewe Hall has provided the setting for hospitality on a grand scale for many leading politicians and leaders of the day, with the highpoint being King George V and Queen Mary's stay in 1913. During the reconstruction of Crewe Hall, Barry added a further extension to the Hall, including the West Wing and the prominent Tower. Having no heirs to the title in 1931, Lord Crewe offered the Hall to Cheshire County Council, who declined the offer. It was later sold to the Duchy of Lancaster in 1936 and remained the property of the Crown until 1998. Occupation by the War Department was part of its use during this time, housing overseas troops from Australia and America - and was used as a prisoner of war camp for over 2,000 high-ranking German Officers. The Welcome Group leased the Hall until 1994 and it was then empty until 1998. The hall was purchased and the transition to a luxury hotel was made. Marston Hotels bought Crewe Hall in July 2003.

Right: The initial letters of the phrase 'Oscar Deutsch Entertains Our Nation' are supposedly the inspiration for the creation of the name that became synonymous with the cinema in the middle of the last century. Deutsch opened his first Odeon in 1930 in his home city of Birmingham, at Perry Bar. By the end of that decade, the cinema chain, often featuring art deco style buildings, was at the forefront of the British entertainment industry. The business continued to flourish after the war, before the downturn in business began in the 1960s as the attractions of television and bingo became major rivals. The Odeon on the edge of Market Square was a handsome building and handily placed close to the bus terminus. Many a young man met his girlfriend off the bus on a Saturday night, enjoyed her company in the quiet seclusion of the two and nines and then walked her back in time to catch the last bus home after a quick kiss goodnight. In 1966, the comedians Morecambe and Wise starred in 'That Riviera Touch'. This was a poor movie about jewel thieves in the south of France and failed to reflect the enormous talents of Britain's top comedy duo. They were tremendous on stage and television, but celluloid was not for them. The Odeon closed its doors in 1983 and was demolished during a redevelopment programme.

Above: The golden age of the cinema took place with the advent of talkies, continuing into the mid 1950s before television reared its rival head and bingo popped up as another competition. Going to the pictures in 1946 was a regular weekly pastime for most of us. Children enjoyed special shows put on just for them and whole families could enjoy two full length feature films, plus several shorts that included comedy sketches, travelogues and newsreels. A night out at the 'flicks' was a full evening's entertainment. Courting couples made full use of the darkened auditorium to get in a couple of hours' worth of canoodling, their amorous couplings punctuated from time to time by the beam of the usherette's torch. Commissioner Norman Tew was in charge of the queuing throngs outside the Empire on High Street. He cut a fine figure, with his light coloured summer uniform that was changed for a green one in winter. The main feature film that brought out the crowds starred Cary Grant, the British born leading man who was a top box office draw in Hollywood movies for over 30 years. 'Night and day' told the story of the composer Cole Porter. Grant co-starred with Alexis Smith, an actress who would later win a Tony award on Broadway and appear in TV's 'Dallas'. The supporting cast included the singer Ginny Simms, musical star Mary Martin, the actor with the trademark white beard, Monty Woolley, and Jane Wymark, the first wife of future President Ronald Reagan. The Empire was demolished in the 1970s and replaced by the new Grand Junction Hotel.

Above: Adelaide School, formerly Adelaide Street Primary School, has been a special state school for secondary aged children since the 1980s. It also spent a short time as a reading centre, a place to where children with some academic problems could come for assessment and assistance. In 1953, it was a more traditional place of learning and here youngsters of all abilities came together to indulge in some practical mathematics in the school yard. The task for this lesson was measuring. Tapes, rulers, yardsticks and the ubiquitous trundle wheels were employed as the kiddies sought to check on height, span and distance. Quite why they had to use the playground to check how far apart Tommy could stretch his legs is something of a mystery. Perhaps the teacher was one of those with a few discipline problems who adopted the approach that 'divide and conquer' was the best policy. Lessons, though, were fairly straightforward for these baby boomers. Mathematics was not a word often used, as arithmetic ruled the day. Tables were learned by heart and chanted out monotonously. Kiddies learned to long multiply and most cottoned on to working in different base numbers as they went from 12 inches to a foot, 16 ounces to a pound and 8 pints to the gallon. Reading was taught via schemes, such as Beacon and Ladybird. The latter set of books featured Peter and Jane, a right pair of prissy individuals.

Below: The picture from the 1960s, shows two barges on the Trent and Mersey Canal at King's Lock, Booth Lane, looking towards Brooks lane and Ashfield Street. The Middlewich Branch from the Shropshire Union Canal arrives in the town from the west. There are two hire boat bases here and the town is a popular stop for boaters.

Petula Clark, (born 15 November 1932), the much loved singer and actress seen here talking to a female worker at Crewe Railway Works in 1949. Clark first performed on radio around 1939, when she was eight. She became known as "Britain's Shirley Temple", and she was considered a mascot by the British Army, whose troops plastered her photos on their tanks for good luck as they advanced into battle. By 1944, Clark was making movies, beginning with "A Medal for the General", ultimately appearing in over 30 British and American films. Though she sang regularly on radio and TV as a child, it wasn't until around the time of this photograph in 1949 that she recorded her first song, "Music, Music, Music. During the 1960s she became known internationally for her popular upbeat hits, including "Downtown" and "Don't Sleep in the Subway". She has sold in excess of 68 million records throughout her career, which has spanned seven decades. In 1998, Clark was honoured by Queen Elizabeth II by being made a Commander of the Order of the British Empire.

Above: The 45 acre Queen's Park site is renowned as one of the finest Parks in the North West. The park is a popular spot for the inhabitants of Crewe and as can be seen in the picture below, also features the largest boating lake in the area. The gas works ash tip provides a rather incongruous background to this 1947 picture of tranquillity on the boating lake at Queen's Park. The spot was known as Tip Kinder Park and used as a BMX bike circuit. It has been renamed as the Shanaze Reade BMX track, after the local woman who has been the sport's world champion. The families happily rowing their ways across the waters would have looked perplexed if you had mentioned BMX to them. They would probably have thought it to be an abbreviation for some form of chemical. Dads who had returned from some far flung battlefield were only too happy to get their life back to normal. Their wives were glad to have them back safe and sound.

Right: Lake Bridge in Queen's Park is just the sport of place to take a short rest and prop your arms on the rails as you interrupt a stroll through one of the most attractive public places in the whole of the northwest of the England. The boating lake is its centrepiece, lying amid handsome grounds, tree-lined walkways and delightful play areas for both young and old. The lake is sourced from Valley Brook and, until 1936, there were bathing huts and a diving board by the west island. Refurbishment in 2010, at a cost of over £6 million, was undertaken to restore the park to its former glory. A combination of National Lottery funding and Cheshire East

investment provided the wherewithal. The land was donated to the people of Crewe by the London and North Western Railway Company. It was dedicated on 4 July, 1887, not in recognition of American Independence Day, but to mark the Golden Jubilee of Queen Victoria's reign. There were tremendous celebrations to mark both the monarch's half century and the opening of the park gates for the first time. Streamers and banners hung along Victoria Avenue and good luck messages were displayed on nearby buildings. A grand procession set off down the avenue through an arch formed by the men of the town's Volunteer Fire Brigade.

They made the arch from ladders, covered in bunting, mottoes and a copy of Crewe's coat of arms.

Above: This scene should be made into a Christmas card. It is such an idyllic view of Crewe's Queen's Park that it makes you wish that winter would never end nor the snows ever melt. Taken in December 1960, this was the month when pop star Adam Faith recorded one of the worst ever Christmas songs. 'Lonely Pup (in a Christmas shop)' was almost too awful for words, but it sold in sufficient numbers to reach number 4 in the charts. And you think modern music is bad?

Right: Does my bottom look big in this? This lass has all the potential for giving lads a tough time. Not only is she very pretty, but she also knows it. Look out, boys. She was obviously well aware of current fashion. Her modern, knitted two-piece was designed more to catch the eye than for practical purposes. The fabric would have got rather heavy and sag somewhat when immersed in the sea. Anyway, she was more interested in making waves among the males on the sands. The first modern two piece was created by Louis Réard in 1946, naming it the bikini after the atoll where atomic bomb tests were carried out. Réard reasoned that the costume's effects would be akin to that of a nuclear reaction and he was not far wrong. It blew some men's brains apart. However, more modest two piece costumes, like the one seen here, had been modelled in the early 1940s by such movie stars as Ava Gardner, Lana Turner and Rita Hayworth.

Below: By the early 20th century, the seaside was a good place to indulge in a little naughtiness as young men showed off their muscles and young ladies displayed flesh that was normally hidden away. You could imagine this pair of young men quite fancied themselves as the type to get girls' pulse racing. Lets face it, which red blooded female would not be driven wild with frenzy at the sight of those knees or the manly pose.

Below and facing page: Jetting off abroad might be all the rage now, but there was a time when getting away meant venturing no further than Lancashire or possibly Wales for local holidaymakers. A straight choice for many between Blackpool or Rhyl, Butlins or Pontins. The golden age of the holiday camp was in the 'fifties and 'sixties. After the War there was a great rush to the coast. Many people had not had a holiday for years and could not wait to get away. The holiday camp provided what they were looking for. Prices were reasonable, food was plentiful and there was plenty to do, even when it was raining. Many families went to the same holiday destination year

after year. But in the 1950s a holiday camp environment was something different, with its knobbly knees competitions, redcoats helping everyone to have fun, and the tannoy system starting each day with the greeting 'Good morning, campers'. Some of the first holiday camps in the UK were the masterplan of entrepreneur William 'Billy' Butlin, who had seen some lakeside holiday centres during a visit to Canada during World War I and realised that they were something that could easily be introduced to his native Britain. Butlin selected the seaside town of Skegness,

war Labour government introduced payed annual holidays for all employees, boosting tourism in the resort. In the 1950s, when holiday camps became fashionable, Blackpool's south shore became the home of 'Pontins'. Extra attractions were added such as Madame Tussaud's Waxworks and bigger and better rides on the Pleasure Beach. During the holiday week it did not matter what the weather did. If you came to the seaside, then you had to sit on the sands. The beach would be jam-packed with people who'd paid twopence for a deckchair. Most of them stayed fully clothed, although a

woman might hitch up her skirt when going for a paddle. Working conditions were extremely hard and people were determined to make the most of their break come what may...even if that meant having a kip on the beach

Lincolnshire, for the location of his first holiday camp, which was opened on 11 April, 1936, by celebrity aeronaut Amy Johnson. The camp was, compared to modern standards, a basic affair. Guests would stay in self-contained prefabricated chalets with three meals a day served in the canteen. But for a country that was recovering from major social upheaval at a global level throughout the 20th Century, the concept of holiday camps was just the tonic to raise Britain's spirits... for a time at least.

Rhyl has long been a popular tourist destination for people all over Wales and North West England and is accessible by road or rail. Once an elegant Victorian resort, there was an influx of people from the North West after World War II changing the face of the town. For years it was a rival to Blackpool, catering for children with open-air attractions like the roller-skating rink, the cycling track and Punch and Judy, along with the landmark Pavilion Theatre, an ornate building with five domes, which was demolished in 1973. But despite Rhyl's popularity, the North Wales resort was never in serious competition with Blackpool in terms of the volume of visitors. In 1938, seven million people reputedly visited Blackpool: that's just under a sixth of the population of England. Another major development came when the post-

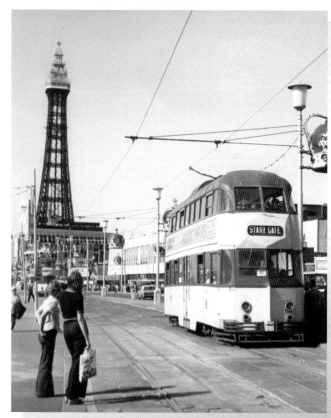

Above: This is an average day to day type of view looking along the A534 Nantwich Road c1960. The vehicles are parked outside the entrance to Crewe Railway Station, which had just completed the reconstruction of a new station entrance. The building to the left in the background is the Crewe Arms Hotel. The building was established in 1880. The Ford Anglia on the left could be a relatively new car as the 105E model was introduced in 1959. A new Anglia saloon tested by the British Motor magazine in the same year, had a top speed of 73.8 mph and could accelerate from 0-60 mph in 26.9 seconds. The test car cost £610 including taxes of £180. It was a time of great excitement as the swinging sixties was just around the corner, Elvis had a No.1 hit in the UK with 'It's Now or Never' and Coronation Street was first aired on TV.

Left: With the Market Street shops providing a backcloth to this photograph, locals sat in the centre of Crewe's Market Square by the war memorial. Some fed the pigeons, but most were just happy to take the weight off their feet. Despite the coats being worn, it seems to have been a fine, warm day. The sun was shining and this was July in 1961. Older women still wore hats when they went into town as they felt that they were not properly dressed if they were bareheaded. Goodness knows what they would think of the 21st century women who appear in the town centre with bare midriffs, sporting pierced navels and all sorts of other adornment.

Above: Now, there's posh. This photograph was taken on 23 December, 1949. Goodness, most people could not afford a radiogram, never mind a television back then. It would not be long, though, before this luxury became an essential part of family entertainment. Until then, an invitation to watch a programme on someone's private set was a privilege. It was the 1953 Coronation and that year's FA Cup Final that helped promote the invasion of the goggle box into all our lives. When those events occurred, people with TVs suddenly discovered that they were the most popular neighbours in the street as locals with whom they had seldom shared a conversation were able to negotiate an invite into the front room. After enjoying the entertainment offered by the splendour of the wedding coach on its way to Westminster Abbey and a seven goal thriller at Wembley, dads were instructed to put television high on the list of goods that they could get on hire purchase. To modern youth the tiny screens and fuzzy pictures would seem hilarious. But, to those of us who were around at the time, it was a magical experience. The kids had Muffin the Mule, Andy Pandy and The Flowerpot Men. Adults watched panel games like 'What's My Line' and exciting drama such as 'The Quatermass Experiment' until the little white dot on the screen faded.

Bottom left: When Ernest Evans asked whether it was a bird or a plane up there and answered himself by telling us that it was a twister, a craze was born that swept dance floors across the western world. He also made sure that countless numbers of children would be embarrassed at weddings, 21st dos and parties during the 1990s as their parents risked hernias and heart attacks attempting to twist the night away whilst their offspring raised their eyes to heaven. Evans was a fan of the 1950s rocker Fats Domino and used his name as the inspiration for becoming

known as Chubby Checker. Oddly, his first big hit in Britain was in 1963 with 'Let's Twist Again', a follow up to 'The Twist', a record that only became very popular the following year. This couple attempted to keep their seams straight as they gyrated in the front room to the music from their Dansette record player,

Below: Graham Haberfield, better known as Jerry Booth from Coronation Street, is seen here during a guest appearance in the Crewe area in 1973. Excited fans lined the street as the 'Corrie' actor arrived at the venue on the bonnet of a Ford Granada. At this time his popularity was high as he was in his third spell in Coronation Street and he will also be best remembered as Winston, the die-hard Manchester City fan in the hit Granada Television sitcom, 'The Dustbinmen'. Haberfield, who was born in Chesterfield in 1941, the son of a railway porter, sadly died suddenly of a heart attack only two years after this photograph was taken.

THE WAR YEARS

Right: No, this is not a scene from Dr Who meets the Cybermen, but something much more real and important. Wearing respirators and protective clothing, these members of the Civil Defence were on exercises in 1941. Although by now people were beginning to realise that chemical warfare might not be an issue in this war, there was no sense in taking chances. After all, many men came back from the First World War suffering the shocking after effects of a mustard gas attack. There had been a real fear that the Nazis would hit our towns with 'dirty bombs' and our home based defenders practised manoeuvres to counteract this threat. Even if such clothing and breathing apparatus was never needed for this purpose, it still; came in useful when fighting fires in factories and bases when poisonous fumes were given off. Readers born in the late 1920s and 1930s will recall carrying their own personal gas masks to school and on the trains and buses taking them away as evacuees in 1939 and 1940. In the background we can see Grice's chemist shop, now Cancer Research UK, and, to the left, Ye Olde Vaults, the pub that dates from the early 1800s. In between, at 46-48 High Street, are houses that date from 1584 and were first occupied by the mercer, Thomas Church, and his nephew, William. They currently belong to the Nantwich Book Shop.

Below: The Women's Land Army (WLA) was a British civilian organisation created during the First and Second World Wars to work in agriculture replacing men called up to the military. Women who worked for the WLA were commonly known as Land Girls. Many women from the county worked on the land or in factories to support the men at the front. Some of the girls were fortunate enough to receive training at places like Reaseheath, an Agricultural College near Nantwich. Once out on the land, life was tough and many land girls were placed on farms that lacked modern amenities of electricity or even running water in some cases. This however, did not deter the girls who worked with great determination and no little humour, to help the war effort.

Above: This section of Crewe's Home Guard paraded impressively in Queen's Park in late 1940, near the pavilion. They drilled with a sense of purpose, particularly happy that they could now boast their own real weapons. Formed as the Local Defence Volunteers in May 1940, these men were the butt of many jokes in their early days. They had little equipment and drilled using broomsticks and came up with fanciful ideas about stringing wire across roads to decapitate any invading Nazi motorcyclist. Made up of some men in reserved occupations, its greatest number included those deemed too young, too unfit or too old to join up. After the initial scorn and lack of supplies had handicapped the force's standing, Winston Churchill took a hand. In July 1940, he was instrumental in having the volunteers renamed as the Home Guard and promoting their importance in the defence of the realm. Proper uniforms and weapons were issued and real military discipline became the norm as the Home Guard took on assigned tasks. It guarded key installations, releasing regular units for more essential duties. Guards were posted at spots likely to be used by invading paratroopers and other personnel manned anti aircraft guns. By the time the units were stood down, men were proud to declare that they had been in dad's army.

Below: This could be a picture from the 1940s of the POW camp off Snape Lane in Weston, near Crewe. At the time of the Second World War there was a prtisoner of war

camp for German and Italian POWs, at Snape Farm, some of whom were put to work on the surrounding farms. Weston POW camp was a camp for ëtrustedí prisoners of war. It was later used to house Polish refugees. Crewe Hall housed Australian and American soldiers, and later became a prisoner of war camp for German officers, during the war.

Below and right: Thanks to television documentaries, we have become well used to seeing action and footage from both world wars that were endured during the last century. Yet, there have been many other occasions in history where Britain lost loved ones on foreign fields. This body of men gathered in Queen's Park to honour those who fell in the Boer or Second South African War (1899-1902) that was fought around the end of Queen Victoria's reign. Seen in front of the war memorial and pavilion that were unveiled in 1903, these men were veterans of that campaign. There are copper bronze plaques on the four sides of the monument that give the names of the railway volunteers who served in the Boer War. Sadly, the pavilion was destroyed by an arsonist in 1970. A 31-foot-high figure of Tommy Atkins tops the

memorial. This name for the common soldier has been attributed to various sources. It was used in a description of a mutiny in the late 18th century. Some say it was claimed by the War Office after the Battle of Waterloo in 1815, but it resurfaced in a poem written by a serving Black Watch soldier in 1899. However, by then Rudyard Kipling had published his poem 'Tommy' as part of his 'Barrack Room Ballads' in 1892 and there followed a popular music hall song entitled 'Private Tommy Atkins'. The paybook issued to all British soldiers in the 1914-18 War used the name 'Tommy Atkins' to illustrate how it should be filled in.

Right: In 1939 Britain's Prime Minister Neville Chamberlain had made his announcement to the waiting people of Britain that '...this country is at war with Germany.' The country rolled up its sleeves and prepared for the inevitable. This war would be different from other wars. This time planes had the ability to fly further and carry a heavier load, and air raids were fully expected. Air raid shelters were obviously going to be needed, and shelters were built on open places across towns and cities. By the time war was declared an army of volunteers of both sexes had already been recruited to form an Air Raid Protection service. It was their job to patrol specified areas, making sure that no chinks of light broke the blackout restrictions, checking the safety of local residents, being alert for gas attacks, air raids and unexploded bombs. The exceptional work done by Air Raid Wardens in dealing with incendiaries, giving first aid to the injured, helping to rescue victims from their bombed-out properties, clearing away rubble, and a thousand and one other tasks became legendary. In July the Local Defence Volunteers was renamed the Home Guard, and by the following year were a force to be reckoned with. Notices went up everywhere giving good advice to citizens on a number of issues. 'Keep Mum - she's not so dumb' warned people to take care what kind of information they passed on, as the person they were speaking to could be an enemy.

Left: War had been declared, and every citizen of Britain, young and old, male and female, was called upon to put his or her back into the war effort. Those who did not go into military service of one kind or another worked in factories, dug for victory, gave up their tin baths and aluminium saucepans, joined organisations and aided in any way they could. These boys were not going to be left out; they might be too young to fight but while there were sandbags to be filled they were going to do their bit to protect their school building. Thousands of sandbags were used during World War II to protect the country and its beautiful civic buildings.

This page: It was possibly the acute wartime shortages of food and supplies made doctors, health workers and mothers alike very aware of the health of the new generation, and children were carefully weighed, measured and immunised against the illnesses that had at one time meant disfigurement or even death. On a day-to-day basis, vitamins were vital to the health of children, and long before the advent of the cod liver oil capsule, the recommended spoonful of cod liver oil was administered to the youngest children every day in schools and nurseries around the country during the 1940s. Children might have screwed up their noses at the fishy taste, but the nourishing cod liver oil went a long way towards keeping them healthy. The vitamin-packed orange juice was far more palatable, and artful mothers would often use the orange juice as a bribe. The photograph below taken in an ante-natal clinic in the 1930s, records at least the cleanliness and tidiness that was to their great credit. And when the tiny new citizen finally arrived, there were health visitors to pay friendly calls on families in their homes to check on the health and happiness of mothers and babies. National Dried Milk for babies was also made available to mothers, and before today's push towards natural feeding NDM was for decades very much in vogue. We need to remember that at the time of these pho-

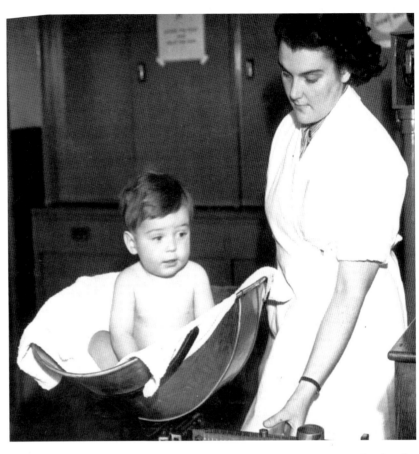

tographs the National Health Service did not exist, and in fact the NHS only came into operation after World War II in July, 1948.

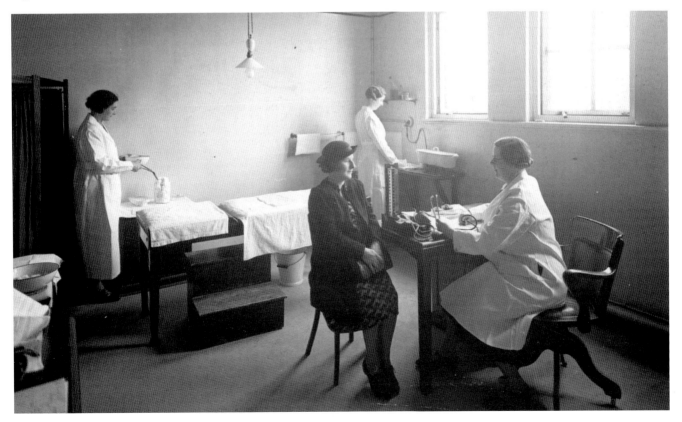

EVENTS & OCCASIONS

Queen Victoria is our longest reigning monarch, coming to the throne in 1837 and continuing to her death in 1901. Queen Elizabeth II will surpass that record in late 2015, God willing. The country rejoiced in

1897 when it was able to mark Victoria's diamond jubilee. Sandbach was just like the rest of the nation, awash with bunting, flags and streamers. Similar scenes were enacted all across the Empire because she was not just our queen, but the ruler of many nations. This was the Victorian age when Britain ruled the waves, controlled foreign lands and dominated world politics. Our influence stretched right the way around the globe and it would take a world war to break our hold on power.

Below: In Winsford, as with every other town and village on the parts of the world map that were coloured red, the month of May in 1910 was greeted with a mixture of sadness and joy. King Edward VII died in the first week of the month, but later on there were celebrations to be had. These took place on Empire Day when we proudly rejoiced in the knowledge that Britannia ruled not just the waves, but many countries besides. Our place as a super power was well established, though such a position would come to an end far sooner than anyone could imagine. Every 24 May was a special occasion. It was the anniversary of Queen Victoria's birthday and was nominated as Empire Day in 1904. It was an appropriate date to choose as it was during her reign that the globe seemed to take on its reddish hue in so many places. There really was a 'Great' in Great Britain. The schoolchildren put on fancy dress and, in later years, the cubs and brownies were permitted to come to school in their uniforms. Union and national flags were flown and the children heard about far off places where the monarch held sway, such as the Gold Coast, Rhodesia, Ceylon and Canada, as well as the even more far flung spots of Tonga, the Solomon Islands and British Honduras. The Commonwealth was officially established in 1931, but we continued to have fun on Empire Day until 1958 when it was renamed.

Right: Simple things kept us amused in Edwardian times. Bowling a ball at a bottle was not the most inventive of games, but it seemed to keep this group of youngsters entertained and the onlooking adults amused. The Wybunbury Garden Party in 1908 was obviously something of a grand affair for the nobs and bigwigs of the district. The cut and style of the suits, hats, bonnets and frocks suggest that those assembled were worth more than a few bob. They were part of what was known as the county set. Even the children were dressed to the nines, looking every inch the little ladies and carbon copies of the Lord Fauntleroys we had read about in Frances Hodgson Burnett's book, published just over 20 years before this scene was enacted. In those times, Britain was still a society where class and high birth counted for a great deal. Our country was divided into those who had wealth and status and those who did not. The First World War would be something of a leveller as men with plummy accents fought and died alongside rougher elements. The machine gun bullets knew no divide as they ploughed their way through ranks of officers and privates alike. That awful conflict was still a few years away when the Wybunbury (pronounced Winbury) gentry met up to enjoy their afternoon of fun. The village is a small backwater, a few miles southeast of Nantwich.

Below: Dressed in all their finery, the Edwardian residents of Willaston had come along to enjoy the village Sports Day. Ladies displayed their best, full length dresses and donned their finest hats and bonnets. Fashion of the day outweighed practicality. Long, floor length dresses were hardly the thing for walking across fields or along dirty streets, but modesty and style counted for more than good sense. Men merely wore whatever looked smart and comfortable. The boater suggested a young beau who was born to one of the fairly high strata of society, while the chap sitting next to him was more down to earth in his flat cap. The young lady leaning on the back of the bench struck a quite coquettish pose, giving the lie to the belief that everything back then was prim and proper. The older woman, to her left, scowled with disapproval. Her attire suggests that she was a widow and her face that she was a humourless one at that. Willaston is situated on the A534, part way between Crewe and Nantwich. It now plays host to the amusing World Worm Charming Championships, a bit of nonsense begun in 1980 that now attracts competitors from all over the globe. It has become a good charity fundraiser and a cheerful way of letting off steam. Comedian Rory McGrath was an entrant in 2008 during filming of a TV series he was making.

Above: The royal train arrived at Crewe Station and King George V and Queen Mary walked along the red carpet to be greeted on the platform by a host of local dignitaries. Mayoral chains, legal wigs and best uniforms were worn with pride for this auspicious occasion. The royal couple did their bit on the fashion front as well. King George sported his smartest top hat and his consort displayed one of the many fine pieces of headgear in her possession. She would become known for some of the most memorable hats, bonnets and headpieces ever displayed by a public figure. Her toques, those colourful, brimless round hats that seemed to reach ever skywards, were something that cartoonists always used when depicting her. The public was quite disappointed if she appeared wearing something else. George and Mary were in town on 21 May, 1913. He had been our monarch for just a fraction over three years, following the death of Edward VII. Mary was born in London, the daughter of a Slav minor royal who was the Duke of Teck. In 1891, she was betrothed to Prince Albert Victor, George's elder brother. However, Albert died shortly afterwards from pneumonia and her affections were transferred to the then Duke of York, largely thanks to matchmaking by Queen Victoria. George and Mary married in 1893. One of the most poignant moments of 20th century royal history took place in 1952. When her son, King George VI, died, Mary was photographed with her daughter-in-law, Queen Elizabeth, and her granddaughter, the new Queen Elizabeth II. Three generations were together in one sad moment.

Right: Foden's has been one of the country's top brass bands for over a century. As a nation, we have a particular liking for this style of music. No heavy industry, mine or mill would have been complete without its own musicians who were able to celebrate the most catholic of tastes from light classical to rousing marches to the show tunes of the era. The top British brass bands are renowned throughout the world for the standard and quality of their concert performances and Foden's are no exception. Its origins can be traced to the village of Elworth that founded a band in 1900 to celebrate the relief of Mafeking during the Boer War. It only lasted for a further couple of years before providing the nucleus for the new Foden's Motor Works Band. By 1909, the members were achieving Championship Section status. In 1913, King George V and Queen Mary visited the works and Edwin Foden commissioned specially made uniforms for band members to wear when they played for their royal guests. These same uniforms were borrowed by men from the joiners' shop who wore them during the Sandbach festival. They mocked up a Zeppelin as the main attraction on the float they paraded as part of the festivities. Foden's is still going strong as a band today, long after the production of lorries ceased in the town.

Above They packed them in as best they could. In 1919, the charabanc trip to New Brighton was going to take a while. With about 20 passengers on board, the average speed the driver could manage was little more than 12 mph. The solid tyres made it a less than luxurious ride, but this was the modern way of doing things. The day trippers put up with inconvenience because they were enjoying the cutting edge of postwar technology. One of the few good things to come out of the Great War was the advancement in motor engineering. The horse was consigned to the knacker's yard and it was all petrol and internal combustion from now on for these doughty pioneers of travel. It was very much the same thing in the skies above them. There, the wonders of air travel and the strides made in such a short time were quite miraculous. In 1909, Bleriot flew the Channel. Just a decade later, Alcock and Brown made it across the Atlantic. Our passengers were only going 45 miles, but it was their adventure. One or two might have warmed up for the journey with a quick snifter in the Castle Hotel on the corner of Heath Street, but most were content to wait until they could have a drink at the Pavilion Theatre on the seaside pier before they took in the show.

umbrella. The first local brigade was formed by the Grand Junction Railway Company in 1843 and the 'fire coupe' was kept under the Chester Road bridge. As the town grew, it became difficult for this appliance to access all parts of the district and the Council was advised to establish its own service. Two brigades, the Crewe Works and the Volunteer, were set up in the 1880s. The Corporation's horse drawn brigade was founded in an empty Methodist chapel in 1892, despite the building being quite narrow in size. A new home at the Corn Exchange on Earle Street was found in 1895 and a steam appliance, still horse drawn, purchased in 1900. A bell in the Market Hall Tower was rung to summon firemen and horse handlers in time of need. A new station was opened on Beech Street East in 1906.

Above: This parade of fire engines, or appliances as the service now likes to call them, rolled along West Street towards Queen's Park. The firemen dressed in their finest ceremonial attire for the occasion and brasses shone brightly, despite the rather damp weather. The display was part of the annual fête held to raise funds for the Cottage Hospital and to heighten the general public's awareness of the good work done by Crewe Fire Brigade. In the 1920s, local authorities supported their own services and it was not until 1941 that the National Fire Service came into being when about 1,600 brigades were brought under one

Below: The town band played lustily in August 1914. It was celebrating, if that is the correct word, the calling up of reservists to join the armed forces in the war that had just been declared with Germany. Excited hordes thronged Nantwich Market Square as young men were encouraged to sign up and take the 'King's shilling'. It was seen as a jolly jaunt by some. Others viewed it as their duty. Women were proud of their sons and husbands who signed up and many were scornful of those who

did not, branding them as cowards and arranging for deliveries of white feathers to be made to their homes. If only they knew what those men were going to have to endure, they might have been a little more reticent to point fingers at those who stayed at home in reserved occupations or delayed signing up until the last moment. It was the war to end wars, but it never did. The whole conflict had its roots in the ambitions of Germany in strengthening its position in the world and the struggle for the upper hand in the Balkans between the forces of the Ottoman Empire and those of Bulgaria, Greece and Serbia. After the assassination of the Austrian Archduke, the domino effect of involving other countries in the dispute became unstoppable.

Above: Every August, a fête has been held in Queen's Park. It was originally arranged to raise funds for Crewe's Cottage Hospital. Since the first Cottage Hospital was opened by Albert Napper in Cranleigh, Surrey, in 1859, the concept spread across Britain and indeed the world. They filled the void between the large voluntary hospitals and workhouse infirmaries in major towns and being nursed in the patients' own homes. They formed the basis for many of today's community hospitals. The fête was preceded by a procession of decorated floats, accompanied by marching bands, dance troupes and a variety of dignitaries in full regalia. A host of local industries were represented, along with departments and workshops from the larger concerns. This shot of West Street in the 1920s shows a bevy of beauty from the CWS clothing factory on Camm Street. These ladies called themselves the 'Spanish Mays'. The parade went from Gresty Road, by the football ground, through the town centre, along West Street before turning into Victoria Avenue and onto Queen's Park. The first such carnival, as the occasion has now become known, took place in the beginning of the last century. Somewhat sadly, a lack of interest meant that the parade through the town had to be scrapped in 2010 for the first time ever; a poor reflection on modern attitudes.

Above: Standing on the edge of The Square, Nantwich, in front of where Holland and Barrett now trade, the Prince of Wales met ex-servicemen from the 1914-18 war during his visit to the town on 20 October, 1926. Large crowds turned out to greet the man who was to be at the centre of the greatest constitutional crisis of modern times. As King Edward VIII he would abdicate the throne in late 1936, just a matter of months after inheriting the crown, and go off into a form of exile with Wallis Simpson, the twice divorced American socialite who turned his head and cost him his birthright. There was no real hint of the major problems that would come his way a decade later, but the prince's compulsive womanising had already raised a few eyebrows in both royal and government circles. He seemed particularly taken with the attractions of ladies who were already married, viewing their conquests with an arrogance that would come to let down his family and the nation.

Bottom left: The war memorial in Market Square was dedicated on 17 June, 1924, to those brave souls who perished in the 1914-18 War. The ceremony was conducted infront of a large crowd who took every vantage point possible, including the balconies on the buildings where Marks & Spencer now stands. The memorial is one of only two in the country that features Britannia. It was erected in this square so that people would pass it on their way to work and spare a thought for those who had made the ultimate sacrifice in the defence of the freedom of their fellows. The unveiling was conducted by General Sir Ian Hamilton in front of 15,000 people who wanted to pay homage to those whose names were writ large on the memorial. The memorial was designed by W Gilbert, of Birmingham, at a cost of £1,600. It was paid for by public subscription. The decision to move it to its current resting place caused a public outcry and resulted in a petition signed by 20,000 locals being presented to the Council. Despite this and the voices raised against the project, the memorial was re-sited in 2006. Much to the disgust of those who wanted it left alone, some damage was caused to it during the move and, to add insult to injury, it was then re-erected the wrong way round.

Below: Every town has its carnival, beauty, May Day or pageant queen. In keeping with its background, Crewe had its Railway Queen. Seen in 1926, this young lady, accompanied by her attendants, performed one of the official duties that came her way during her year of office. It was Remembrance Day and she laid a wreath at the foot of the War Memorial on behalf of everyone gathered in the crowd who had come to pay their respects to those who died in the Great War.

Below: Just because there was a war on did not mean that certain traditional occasions had to be abandoned. The Olde Boote Shoppe, in Sandbach, provided the backdrop for the annual Whit Walk in 1940. Parading in a new set of clothes and collecting cash from assorted uncles and aunts was a feature of life in those days. The religious significance of the Whit festival was rather lost in the excitement of showing off your finery, like some pleased peacock. Despite that, wearing your Sunday best was important to us as a sign that work was done for the week and here was a particular day to be recognised. The parade through town meant more to mums and dads than it did to the children, some of whom were rather overcome by the whole thing. From the earliest days of Christianity, Pentecost or Whitsun was set aside in northern Europe as one of the days in preference to Easter when Baptism could be celebrated as a sacrament. Perhaps this was because the temperature was likely to be a few degrees warmer and less traumatic for those indulging in full-water immersion for the ceremony. The word 'Whit' is probably derived from the practice of baptismal candidates and the clergy in donning white clothing and vestments as a sign of purity. Though also supported by Anglicans, the Whit Walks were largely associated with the Catholic Church and statues and images of the Blessed Virgin being borne aloft were often features of the parades.

Above: We got used to street parties during the 20th century. We celebrated glad affairs, such as coronations and those that marked the passing of the days of turmoil as in the ending of two wars with Germany and the one with Japan. Additionally, the British took note of jubilees. This 'do' was held on the former Sandbach Street in May, 1935, in honour of the silver jubilee of King George V. It looks to have been a very orderly affair, with vases of charming flowers, decent crockery and starched tablecloths adorning the various living room tables that had been pressed into service. The terraced housing was festooned with streamers and jolly bunting and the kiddies peeked out at the camera from under paper hats many had made with the help of their mothers. Two years later and the same furniture, albeit with a fresh supply of blooms, would be used again in recognition of the coronation of George VI. There were to be no more jubilees until 1977 and 2002, when milestones in the reign of our present monarch were celebrated.

until the 2008 by-election when voters rejected the candidacy of Tamsin Dunwoody. She was attempting to continue the family connection with this seat that her mother, Gwyneth, began in 1974 until her death 34 years later. However, the voters preferred change to some form of inheritance.

Bottom left: The 1939 Carnival Queen and her attendants were taken on a tour of the Crewe Locomotive Works by members of the erecting shop staff. The pretty faces stood out amidst the sea of boiler suited males. They would not have much to cheer about over the next six years as the lights went out, the balloon went up and we readied ourselves for another bitter conflict with our German foes.

Below: As usual, Queen Elizabeth was prominent during the royal visit in 1940. The stop at Crewe was part of a national morale lifting exercise. Locals were thrilled to see the woman who steadfastly refused to run and hide in Canada or some other far corner of the world when the Germans were blitzing our homeland. Her husband, King George VI, was a reticent, shy man and Elizabeth was more than able to cover for him and to be the sort of public persona of the Windsor family that he found difficult to adopt. Her winning smile and determination won her many friends. Typically, here she made a beeline for a member of the support services, rather than giving her attention to those sporting chains and top hats. Well done ma'am. She was destined to spend half a century as a widow and the public took her to its heart in a way it did for few royals in the 20th century.

Above: Crewe North/Central Ward Labour Party was holding a rally in 1934. This was the time of the Depression when large numbers were out of work, especially in the larger industrial areas. The British Labour Party was still a fairly new body, having been founded in just 1900. Even so, it had major success in the polling booths after the First World War. J Ramsey MacDonald was the leader of two minority governments in 1924 and 1929-31. He also served as prime minister of the coalition National Government, 1931-35. Sir David Somervell (Conservative) was Crewe's MP at the time of this gathering. He lost his seat to Labour in the 1945 Attlee landslide and the Tories were in the cold in Crewe and Nantwich

Above: These youngsters are about to have a whale of a time. But, note that there are hardly any young men to be seen as they are still waiting to be demobbed. This is to be a party for women, children and grandparents, in addition to those dressed up as Beefeaters. Celebrations to herald VE Day, when the end of hostilities in Europe was announced on 7 May, 1945, would also be repeated on 14 August for VJ Day. With the victory over Germany secure, we were ready to let our hair down. After nearly six years of trial and turmoil, we could relax as all over the country trestle tables were pulled out onto the pavements. Coloured strips of cloth were hung from lamposts and flags fluttered across window sills. Schoolrooms and church halls lent their tables and benches, dining room chairs appeared outside the front door and the street parties began in earnest. Neighbours had become even more reliant on each other during the years of deprivation. With rationing biting hard, they helped out with the loan of a cup of sugar or an outgrown frock. Now they were getting together to give their children the time of their lives. Hoarded ration coupons were pooled as sandwiches were filled, cakes baked in the oven and homemade orangeade appeared as if by magic. The best drawer in the sideboard was raided for tablecloths and

excited kiddies sat down and tucked in. Some mums shed a silent tear for the men who would not be coming home, but joined in with the rest to welcome a brighter and better world. In the background are examples of prefabs, those easy to erect homes that appeared in the mid and late 1940s as replacement housing, mainly for those who had been bombed during the Blitz. Even though intended as a temporary measure, many remained in use for decades and a handful are still to be seen in use today.

Bottom Left: The Sea Cadets had already celebrated Queen Elizabeth's Coronation in June and now they were called into action once more as part of the parade in August, 1953, Crewe Fête. The lads marched proudly along West Street, as well they should. They were members of the oldest, continuous youth organisation in the United Kingdom. The Sea Cadet Corps dates to 1854 when a clergyman who returned from the Crimean War was saddened to find so many orphaned boys with bereaved mothers who had lost their loved ones at Inkerman, Sebastopol, Alma, Balaclava and other fields of conflict. With the help of sailors returning from the war, an orphanage was established in Whitstable. By the end of the 19th century, a number of 'Brigantines' had been set up in many towns, somewhat loosely organised as 'Naval Lads' Brigades'. The Navy League, a pressure group formed in 1895 to influence maritime thinking in government circles, supported these brigades to the extent that it was sponsoring 34 of them by the time war was declared in 1914. The Navy League Sea Cadet Corps gained its official name in 1919. By the start of the next war, there were 100 such units, with 10,000 members, spread across the country. Today, Sea Cadets are aged from 12 to 18, though 10 and 11 year olds can be affiliated as Junior Sea Cadets.

Below: Cherry Tree Road is a cul-de-sac to the north of Crewe town centre, part of one of those housing estates that planners decided just had to have a themed name. Consequently, this road is surrounded by titles that include lime, ash, sycamore and elm. However, Prunus Road, Sorbus Drive and Pyrus Avenue really do demonstrate that someone had an in-depth knowledge of all matters woody. The photograph was taken as the Cherry Tree Road baby boomers celebrated the 1951 Festival of Britain. These kiddies were born during the war or in that period immediately after when the birth rate really took off. The stork put in a claim for overtime and a whole new generation that would provide the impetus for the changes in the swinging 60s came into being. The Festival of Britain was the Labour government's idea to bring a bit of joy into what was known as 'austerity Britain'. A national exhibition, celebrating everything that was good about the United Kingdom, was just what the doctor, or more exactly Herbert Morrison, ordered as a 'tonic for the nation'. The Festival helped shape 1950s' architecture, blending modernism with English eccentricity, and even gave some inspiration to such architects as Basil Spence, who went on to design Coventry Cathedral in the early years of the following decade. The kiddies knew naught of this; they just liked a party. Some had not had one before and the others only had faint memories of those held on VJ and VE Days.

Below: During a tour of the Works, Crewe Railway workers congratulate LMS (London Midland Scottish) employee Beatrice Mary Rhead on her election as Crewe's Locomotive Queen for 1936. The London, Midland and Scottish Railway Company (LMS) came into being on 1 January, 1923, as a result of the amalgamation of more than 300 smaller railway companies into the "Big Four". Besides being the world's largest transport organisation, it was also the largest commercial undertaking in the British Empire and the United Kingdom's second largest employer, after the Post Office.

Above: On 26 April, 1952, the last steam locomotive to be seen near Wheelock was surrounded by enthusiasts. They had come from far and wide to pay homage to one of those magnificent feats of engineering that had put Britain at the forefront of rail development. We have a proud history in this country when it comes to steam engines. It was on the Stockton and Darlington line that goods were first moved

in 1825. In 1829, Stephenson's Rocket won the Rainhill passenger railway trials held by the Liverpool and Manchester Railway Company. The scene was now set for nigh on 150 years. In the inter-war years of the 20th century, speed records were broken almost at a whim. Locomotives with evocative names, such as the Cheltenham Flyer, Flying Scotsman, Silver Jubilee and Coronation Scot, kept the public fascinated with records that defied belief. Yet, it was the unremarkably named Mallard, a conventional Class A 4-6-2 Pacific model, built in Doncaster, that set a world record for steam locomotives that still stands today. Designed by Nigel Gresley, in 1938 it exceeded 125 mph. Fancy having such a record held by a duck! Our fascination for steam continues today, with the organisers of weddings, 21st birthday parties and works outings all clamouring to hold their celebrations in the carriages of a train pulled by a restored loco on a line that has been lovingly brought back to life.

Below: The rain did not keep the crowds away in 1955 when Queen Elizabeth II paid Crewe a visit. Hats were doffed and flags waved as the local population cheered the motorcade through town. This was a time when the nation hoped that a new Elizabethan age was upon us. It seemed fitting that we had a young woman on the throne for she could represent the dawn of a new era for us. The previous half century had brought little but woe, with its two world wars, a decade of depression and years of postwar austerity. Perhaps this was the time when we could burst forth from the gloom and enter a brighter tomorrow. Rationing had finished at long last and our industry's order books were filling up. It did seem that there was some form of lightening of the skies on the horizon. Here in front of us was a youthful mother of two who could understand our concerns for the wellbeing of our families. Perhaps she could help our government put the 'Great' back into Britain once more.

Right: Our new monarch was in town and her subjects showed their loyalty as they lined the streets, patiently waiting for the motorcade to pass. They would only get a fleeting glimpse of the young woman who, in 1955, was not yet 30 years of age and had only been crowned as Queen Elizabeth II a couple of years earlier. Many schoolchildren were granted a half day holiday so that they could cheer Her Majesty as she waved regally at them from the back seat of her limousine. The little tots carried streamers on sticks and tiny Union flags that they waved with great gusto. One little girl in the foreground displayed some Australian connections, by the look of the flag that she brandished. Most of the men were at work as this was still an age when the male was the breadwinner and the female played the part of the homemaker. Being a housewife was regarded as an important role in the family. These mums wrapped up

against the chill and rain, put on their headscarves and hats and shared a kerbside with mothers of like views. They were happy with their lot and proud to be British with a royal family to cheer.

Right: Born on 4 August, 1900, Elizabeth Bowes-Lyon graced the whole of that era before passing away on 30 March, 2002. What things she saw. She came onto this earth as a Victorian when man could only leave the ground by balloon. By the time she was middle aged, he was playing golf on the moon. Her world of communications was limited to telegraph and telephone. Within her span, we saw cinema, radio, television, satellites and the internet take centre stage, all in turn. Around her, the world endured two global wars and the map she first observed, dominated by British imperial red, turn into many different colours. Her

homeland altered from being a major power to one with reduced influence on the wider stage. As a young woman she spent much of her early life in Glamis, Angus, and her ancestral home became a convalescent hospital for wounded soldiers during the First World War. After the Armistice, she moved to join the London set that surrounded the royal family. The Duke of York, Prince Albert, proposed to her on several occasions before she accepted marriage to him and they sealed the knot in 1923. She endeared herself to the nation when she placed her bridal bouquet on the Tomb of the Unknown Soldier on her way to Westminster Abbey. In November, 1968, she was now well established as the 'Queen Mum', having been widowed over 16 years earlier. On her official visit to Crewe she was greeted by the Mayor, Alderman Wilf Talbot, and his wife, Mayoress Sheila Talbot.

SHOPPING SPREE

The Black Bear, in Sandbach, provided the backdrop for this view of the market in full swing in the very first years of the 1900s. No doubt many a hubby made the excuse to pop into the public bar for something to wet his whistle while the missus went off to do the shopping. At least he offered to carry the bags home, provided he had not tarried too long and was still capable of walking in a straight line. Despite some important connections with industry, much of East Cheshire has been more at home with its links to agriculture and the rural community. We can more readily identify with this picture than with those of smoking factory chimneys. Ye Olde Black Beare Inn was formerly owned by Lord Crewe. Built in 1634, the timbered black and white pub is one of the town centre's landmarks and the only one still to boast a thatched roof. Located at the entrance to the market square, there is little doubt that the so-called sport of bear baiting was practised on or near this spot. Its popularity began in Tudor times and herds of bears were maintained for this purpose. Special arenas known as bear gardens, as opposed to beer gardens, were established, often close to hostelries such as the one pictured. Remarkably, the cruel practice was not officially outlawed in Britain until 1835. The highwayman Dick Turpin is thought by some to have stayed at the Black Bear, but virtually every inn up and down the land makes a similar, unreliable claim.

Below: This was shopping, Edwardian style. The elegant mother on the left, pausing in front of the General Drapery Establishment at Britannia House in 1908, was well dressed as befitted a lady of her times. She strolled along Victoria Street, away from Market Street, with her children for company as she took in what was on offer in the various stores and emporia along the road. No self respecting lady appeared in town unless she was able to look smart. Dress with a degree of formality was required, because one never knew who she might meet. It would not do to be talked about in the parlours of polite society and later find out that the side had somehow been let down. The lads behind her had their own ideas of what they should wear, or at least their parents did. They looked just like smaller, younger versions of their dads. They all wore jackets and shirts, along with, in some cases, flat caps. It would be many decades before young men adopted a style of their own. The bus trundled away, laden with passengers on the draughty top deck, passing the music shop where pianos and organs were on sale. Many homes, even modest ones, boasted that they possessed a simple piano, at least. Someone in the family could be relied upon to 'tickle the ivories' and produce a passable rendition of a popular music hall number. Radios and record players were still to come and people made their own entertainment. The Brooklyn pianos on sale were probably produced by Green and Savage of London and it is doubtful if the examples on sale in Crewe had ever ventured as far as New York, despite their name. B Squire's piano company was established in 1829, being taken over by Kemble's in the 1930s. The American Estey organs being advertised were manufactured in Vermont and their sale would have been restricted to the middle classes with substantial means.

Right: Market Day in Sandbach was a noisy, busy occasion in the early 1900s, just as it had been for many centuries before. The name of the town means sandy stream or valley and traces of a settlement can be found that date to Saxon times. However, it did not become an official market town until the Tudor era when Elizabeth I granted a charter in 1579 to establish a Thursday market. Sandbach's new status was achieved after much lobbying at court by Sir John Radclyffe, of Ordsall, a prominent local landowner. The town could also hold two annual fairs, at Easter and in

September. Today, an outdoor market is still held on a Thursday on Scotch Common and the indoor market under the Town Hall is open on Thursdays and Saturdays. The cobblestones on Market Square, across to the Crown, were covered with stalls and barrows selling their wares in this picture of life that dates back over a hundred years. As traders and stallholders pressed fruit and vegetables into the hands of eager shoppers, horse drawn vehicles drifted by. Piles of droppings were scattered over the square, but no health and safety officials rushed onto the scene. There was no evidence of polythene gloves being used when handling food or hands being cleaned with some form of antiseptic gel; yet we survived and even thrived.

Right: Nantwich cobbler TH Sley posed with several family members in the shop doorway. Taken in 1900, the year of the Relief of Mafeking, the photograph shows how small family businesses were run from premises that could also double up as homes. There would be a room at the back that served as a kitchen and living room, while the sleeping quarters were upstairs. Dependent on how many children there were was also the answer to how many slept to a bed. The toilet, of course, was out in the back yard, along with the tin bath hanging off a nail hammered into the wall. Cobbling was an important trade. Members of the working classes could not afford umpteen

pairs of shoes or boots. They had one pair for work and another for best. When a shoe wore down or a sole wore through then it was round to the cobbler's for mending. New ones were a luxury. Sometimes, even a repair had to wait if money was on the short side. Then a piece of cardboard shoved inside the shoe did as a sole until pay day came along. Mr Sley had never heard of designer trainers. The only trainers he knew were the ones who ran onto the pitch carrying a sponge at Gresty Road whenever one of Alex's players took a knock.

Below: The photographer's position on the edge of Oat Market in late Edwardian Nantwich is easily recognisable to modern eyes. The view along this section of High Street, towards where WH Smith now trades, has changed little in the intervening years. We now have the Cheshire and Britannia Building Societies, the British Heart Foundation and Pinnington's optician shop on the left, but it all looks quite familiar, above the shop façades especially. Over to the right, we now call in at the Edinburgh Woollen Mill shop or Reed's estate agency, but one constant continues to dominate this patch of the town. The Crown Inn, a Grade I listed building, was erected close to the site where a Norman castle once stood. A major fire badly damaged much of the heart of the town in 1583 and Queen Elizabeth I contributed financially towards its rebuilding. A number of Nantwich's historic buildings, including this fine coaching inn, date from late Elizabethan or early Stuart times. The Crown is thought to date from 1584-5 and was used as a place of worship during the Civil War. An assembly room was added at the rear in the 1700s. It was a coaching inn on the London to Chester run.

Above: Being a bobby on point duty on the corner of Victoria Street with Market Street was not too bad a job in 1930. There was not too much traffic to trouble the boy in blue on Crewe's streets in 1930. Motorcars were very much the province of the middle classes and the boom times for ownership by the masses were still over a quarter of a century away. Still, our uniformed friend had to be alert to keep vehicles, both motorised and horse drawn, on the move in a safe and efficient manner. Although traffic was light, the streets were becoming ever more dangerous for pedestrians, especially the older generation unused to the speeds that cars and lorries could achieve as they whizzed around corners. Electrically controlled traffic lights had only just started to appear on our roads and it would be some time before they became the norm at busy junctions. Until then, we had to rely on the bobby helping us make our way safely and upon our own awareness of the new dangers with which we had to contend. As the 1930s unfolded, Britain gained the most unenviable record of having one of the worst set of statistics for injuries and deaths on the road in the whole of Europe. Until 1935, there was not even such a thing as a driving test to be passed. Much of the right hand side we see here is now occupied by such stores as The Works and Specsavers, with an entrance to The Market Shopping Centre level with the policeman, also on the right. He is now superfluous as the area is restricted to pedestrians who frequent such places as Body Shop, Regis and 3 Store that are names not heard of when Crewe's answer to PC49 pulled on his uniform.

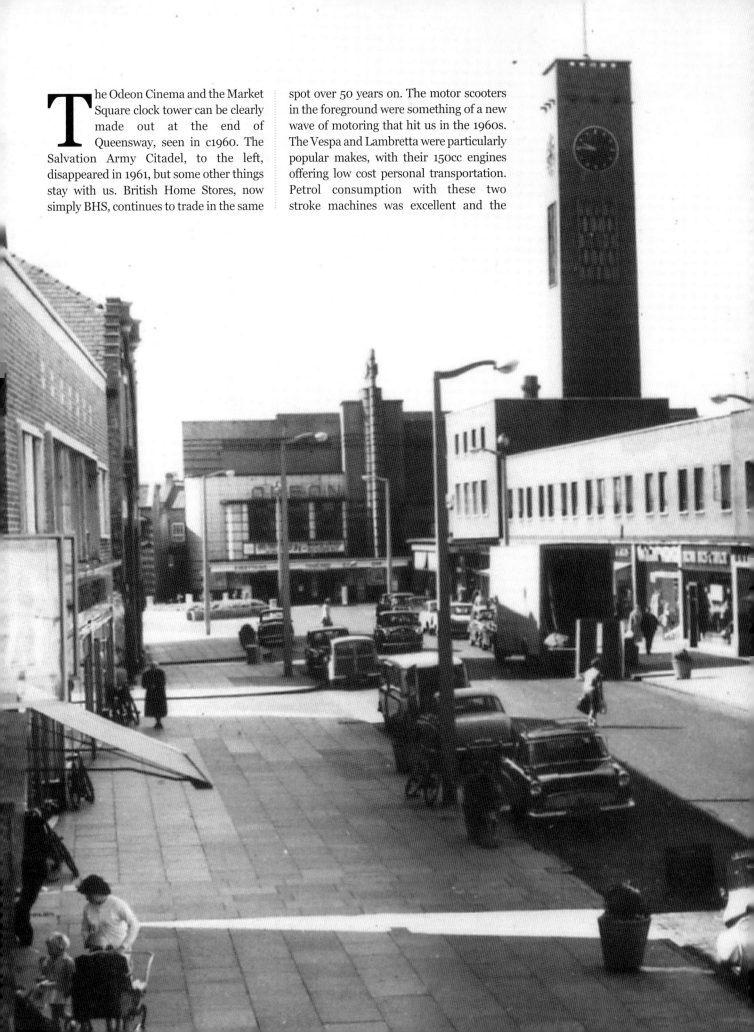

The Odeon Cinema and the Market Square clock tower can be clearly made out at the end of Queensway, seen in c1960. The Salvation Army Citadel, to the left, disappeared in 1961, but some other things stay with us. British Home Stores, now simply BHS, continues to trade in the same spot over 50 years on. The motor scooters in the foreground were something of a new wave of motoring that hit us in the 1960s. The Vespa and Lambretta were particularly popular makes, with their 150cc engines offering low cost personal transportation. Petrol consumption with these two stroke machines was excellent and the

Italian connection that the manufacturers offered gave a trendy, continental flavour to scooter ownership. In the middle of the 1960s they were especially favoured by groups of young people who called themselves 'mods' and wore fur lined, long anoraks, sported flowing hair and listened to music by the Small Faces. Their rivals were the 'rockers' who favoured powerful motorbikes, black leathers and still regarded Gene Vincent, Eddie Cochran and Jerry Lee Lewis as their musical gods.

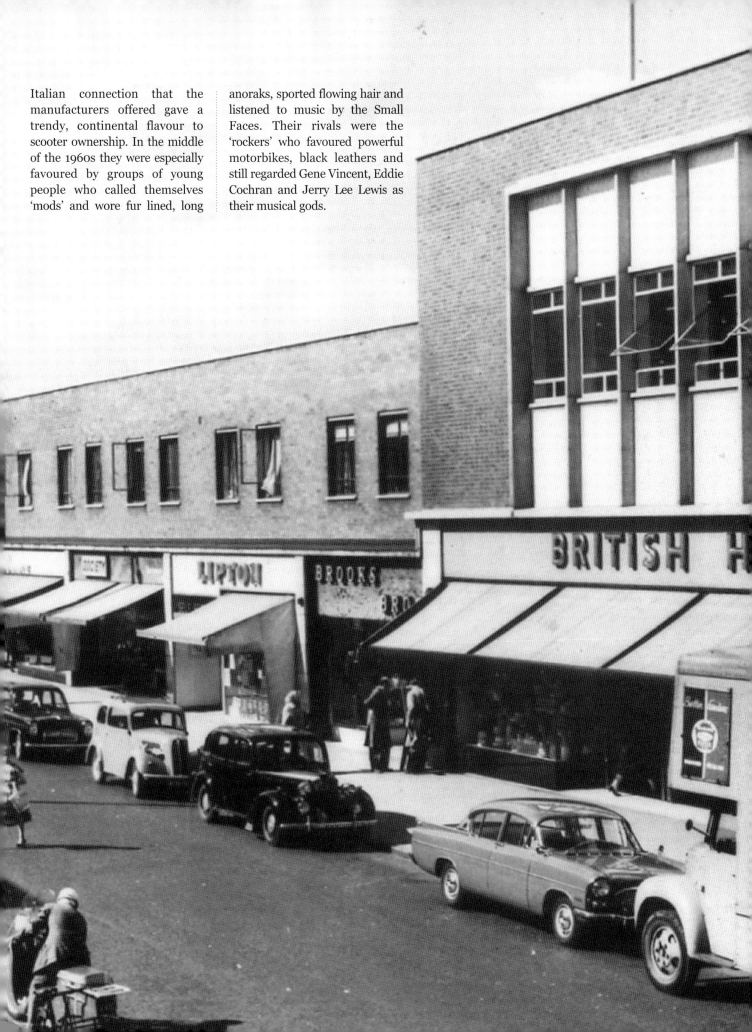

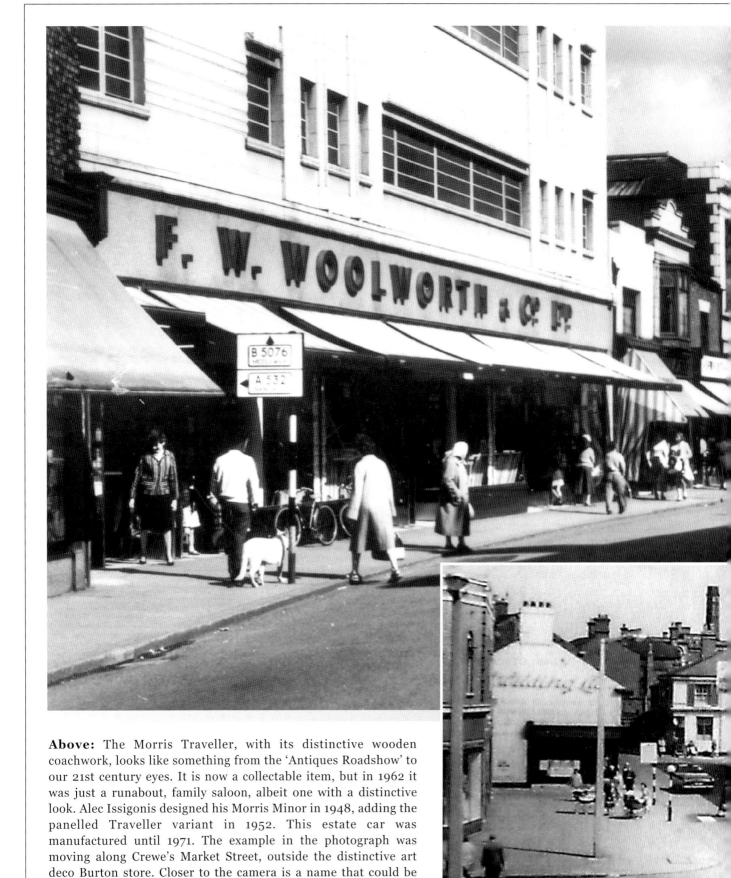

Above: The Morris Traveller, with its distinctive wooden coachwork, looks like something from the 'Antiques Roadshow' to our 21st century eyes. It is now a collectable item, but in 1962 it was just a runabout, family saloon, albeit one with a distinctive look. Alec Issigonis designed his Morris Minor in 1948, adding the panelled Traveller variant in 1952. This estate car was manufactured until 1971. The example in the photograph was moving along Crewe's Market Street, outside the distinctive art deco Burton store. Closer to the camera is a name that could be found in almost every town in the land until a few years ago. FW Woolworth, the five and ten cent store founded in America in

1878, was a major and surprise casualty of the recession that hit in the final years of the last decade. The 'Wonder of Woolies', as a television advertisement once described the shopping experience, was lost forever. Its demise was swift and complete. In the background right of this picture is The Grand Junction Inn which was a well named Crewe watering hole. It stood on the corner of Heath Street where Market Street and Victoria Street meet up. The cyclist waiting patiently at the traffic lights in 1963 has no need to worry about amber gamblers and one way streets as the area is now for pedestrians only. The inn was demolished to make way for the Market Centre and a replacement pub of the same name was built just a few yards away.

Below: It was quiet in town on this day in the late 1950s. This part of Crewe has altered quite dramatically in modern times. Victoria Street's shopping area is pedestrianised and remodelled, with the left hand side of what we can see now dominated by The Market Shopping Centre that was completed in 1998. Love it or loathe it, the new style of shopping has done away with what we can see here and condemned it to the memory banks.

Crewe's Victoria Street on 21 September, 1963, was alive with shoppers in the days before large malls and a multitude of supermarkets began to rule the roost. For those of us of more senior years, it hardly seems like nearly half a century since we popped out to the shops and paid a visit to Ashley's for our wallpaper and other decorating essentials. Nowadays, you would get it all from some mammoth superstore that also sold plants and lawnmowers and did a little catering on the side. It seems for all the world that the days of the dedicated shop are largely over.

Above: Britain underwent a period of social change in the 1960s. Mum and dad were out and young people were in. Their lifestyles became important factors in everything from the retail world to that of moral values. There was a more relaxed mood in the air and this initially transmitted itself in the way people dressed. Going into town was not quite the formal affair it once had been. Women dressed much more casually and left their hats at home. Men went out and about in sloppy cardigans and corduroy trousers. Skirt lengths started to creep higher, along with male pulse rates.

Young men went from school to work or higher education without having to take time out for National Service in the armed forces. Young women went looking for training and opportunities for further learning and advancement, rather than accepting that a factory job and marriage were the next steps in their lives. Grice's became a chemist, not a druggist, and cafes changed to coffee houses. Bob Dylan sang to us that 'the times they are a-changing' and how right he was.

Bottom left: Only the names on the shops have changed on the High Street, Nantwich, since this photograph from the 1960s was taken. Looking along the right hand side, opposite The Square, we now call in at M and Co., Chatwin's coffee lounge, Cancer Research UK, Nantwich Book Shop and Ye Olde Vaults. Across the way, we have WH Smith, Holland and Barrett, Supernews and The Works. Supernews is one of those buildings built after the fire in the 16th century that gutted the town centre. Elizabeth I helped fund the rebuilding and a plaque on this building reads 'God grante our ryal queen in England longe to raign for she hath put her helping hand to bild this town again'. This may not be the original sign and the spelling deliberately made archaic, but we get the message.

Below: Most of Market Street is forbidden to cars these days, so shoppers can wander along it in safety. In 1963, they had to stay firmly on the pavement, which was easier said then done on a crowded Saturday in the heart of town. Still, if you got separated from your companion it was always a good idea to have a pre-arranged meeting place. Burton's corner has long been a popular, well known spot and always a good choice as everybody knows its location. Crewe's 'tailor of taste' is just one of many outlets of the chain that blossomed in the inter-war years of the last century. The stores were named after the founder who, in turn, had taken his name from the Staffordshire town just 45 miles from here. Moshe Osinsky, a Lithuanian Jew, came to England in 1900. After working as a peddler in Manchester, he opened a general outfitter's shop in Chesterfield, using his adopted name of Montague Burton as it sounded more British. He did not make the change official and this was to cause him problems during World War I as he was classed as an alien. By the start of that conflict, he had five shops selling ready to wear men's clothing. During the 1920s, the expansion of his company was dramatic. It seemed that a new outlet was opening on a High Street in some British town almost every week. By the end of that decade he had 400 links to his chain.

ON THE MOVE

The omnibus belonging to the Nantwich and Crewe Motor Bus Company was parked up in The Square. This was the first of the motorised public transport vehicles used by the company. Sporting the registration mark M878, it commenced

taking business on 15 July, 1905. It is possible that this is a photograph of the inaugural journey as the ladies and gentlemen on the open top deck were dressed in all their finery. The best dresses and most resplendent of headgear were displayed by the fairer sex and their escorts included several who had brushed up their top hats especially for the occasion. A couple of them had brushed up their side whiskers as well. If this was not the first ever run, then in must have been an important occasion as people who could afford to dress in such a manner would hardly have deigned to travel by public transport and certainly would not have exposed themselves and their finery to the elements.

Below: The Victorians had a particular penchant for naming things after famous people and important events. Dotted across the country you will find streets such as Inkerman Terrace and Mafeking Walk, recalling Battles in the Crimea and South Africa. There are also many parts of towns named in the middle of the 19th century for heroes from the earlier Georgian era, such as Nelson Place and Wellington Square. When it came to thinking of names for magnificent examples of British engineering, then our

forefathers again looked for figures of importance and/or high birth for their inspiration. Here we have the 'Alfred Paget'. The original of this locomotive was built in July, 1865, as a 0-4-2ST model. It was rebuilt and remodelled by Webb's in December, 1897. Lord Alfred Paget (1816-88) was the fourth son of the Marquis of Anglesey and a director of the North Staffordshire Railway Company. His family decided to branch out into coal mining in the middle of the 19th century. The Pagets leased some mines out to others, including the Cannock Chase Colliery Company that ran ten pits in the Chasewater area. The pictured locomotive continued in colliery service until scrapped by the National Coal Board in 1952. However, the Paget name has been preserved in use on a Neilson engine operated by the heritage railway that runs in Chasewater Country Park on the edge of the reservoir.

Above: Today's Health and Safety Executive would've had eggs in the old days! 'Bunking' engine sheds was fraught with danger. Young boys, barely knee-high to a grasshopper dodged locomotive movements in the shed yard, leaped over inspection pits without any thoughts of the risks involved. All around, railwaymen went about their everyday business – too busy to be chasing spotters off the premises – which made the danger no less real. Jim Carter's atmospheric shot of a busy Crewe North Shed evokes all manner of 'spotting' memories.

Below: Nantwich Road seems a much narrower thoroughfare today than it was in 1903. That can only be a trick of the light, or perhaps it is because modern road markings mean that cars have no space in which to overtake one another. The magnificently styled Brunswick Hotel on the left was a most handsome affair. There is still a pub here of the same name, but it was redeveloped some decades ago and looks much more functional than its more ornate ancestor. Further along to the right, by Gresty Road, the Royal Hotel continues to dispense fine ales. The dray heading from the direction of the junction with Mill Street paused for a moment as the driver checked to find how many barrels of beer he needed to deliver. These wooden casks gave the liquor a distinctive, nutty flavour, far removed from the gassy, light coloured stuff forced out of dispensers on the counters of 21st century bars. The dray would then be off to the brewery, further along Nantwich Road. The bus passengers, shortly to be passing Edleston Road, were probably Nantwich bound. Piled precariously high on the top deck and squashed inside, the passengers were quite happy with a little bit of sardine style travel. Walking to Crewe's neighbouring town would have taken a good hour and a half, but the bus could do the journey in no more than 20 minutes. The world was getting smaller.

Right: The Market Square acted as Crewe's bus terminus until around 1960. Here, in 1938, we can see how busy a spot this was with passengers hurrying and scurrying across to the place where they could start their ride home from work or an afternoon at the shops. The war memorial and the handsome, ornate lamp standards added a touch of class to the scene that would not be to the taste of architects who came along 30 years later and determined that everything had to be rectangular and purely functional. Single decker buses dominated the scene and the one in the foreground shows a particularly interesting feature, especially for younger readers. They may wonder why the bus has a handle sticking out of the front. Older readers may now regale them with tales of hand cranking engines on cold days in order to get them to fire up. Mum or one of the taller children used to sit behind the driving wheel ready to press the accelerator pedal when the engine threatened to cough into life. The assistant had to be careful not to flood the engine or to accidentally move the gear lever and see hubby or dad squashed against the wall. Even buses sometimes needed a helping hand to get going. The Crosville Motor Company was the name in omnibus provision in our area from the early days of motorised public transport. The Council gave its approval to Crosville to

provide services between Crewe, Middlewich and Nantwich in December, 1913. Two years later, a foothold in the town itself was gained with the acquisition of Ward Brothers, a company that had provided horse-drawn passenger transport since about 1900. Crosville expanded its fleet of Daimler CK chassis vehicles with the addition of new Leylands in 1921. A dozen Leyland Leviathan double deckers were purchased in 1926. During the 1930s, Crosville consolidated its position as the leading bus operator in North Wales, Cheshire and the Wirral.

Below: The branch line and Middlewich station were built by the London and North Western Railway (LNWR) during 1867-1868. The railway line was completed in November 1867 and was initially used by goods trains. The station was completed later and was opened for passenger use on 1 July 1868. With the growth in car usage and competition from improved bus services, Middlewich station shared in the common experience of a decline in railway passengers. The station became an early victim of the British Railways closure programme, with regular passenger trains ceasing to use the branch on 4 January 1960. The Mid Cheshire Rail Users' Association has campaigned for the reintroduction of passenger services on the Sandbach - Northwich line and the construction of a new station at Middlewich.

Below: The final batch for 10 'Britannias' Nos 70045-70054 were ordered with type BR1D tenders carrying 9 tons of coal and 4725 gallons of water. This was one of the LMR's longest serving titled trains which operated between Euston and Holyhead to connect with sailings to Ireland. Here, No 70054 Dornoch Firth 9 delivered September 1954, withdrawn November 1966, ambles past Crewe workshops.

Right: Even at this young age, maybe this tot was destined to drive a classic tourer seen in the picture bottom right. Little pedal cars were all the rage, especially for young boys, in the 1930s. Motoring was booming and toy manufacturers spotted the opportunity of a new niche in the market. While less affluent parents bought their children scooters for Christmas, Santa Claus packed his sleigh with imitations of real motorcars for the offspring of the wealthy. Some cars actually featured windows

that moved, working horns and lights, real chrome, bonnet ornaments, white wall tyres and custom paint. Many of the cars were made from metal, though this became less likely in the 1940s as the war effort demanded that such materials were channelled into the manufacture of military ordnance.

Below: Author Kenneth Grahame (1859-1932) is best remembered for his 1908 book 'Wind in the Willows'. The driver of this 1933 car might just have been modelled on Mr Toad. It is certainly the type of tourer that would have got the old boy's heart racing, as well as the engine. He would happily speed along the lanes, shouting 'What fun!' and fun it must have been in real life for the owner of such a car. Britain's roads were not cluttered with traffic as they became later on and it was easy to find an open stretch of road and just let rip. This fine example of craftsmanship, was registered in 1933. Younger readers might look at the front of the car and observe a small hole at the bottom of the radiator grille and wonder as to its use. This was where a starting handle was inserted and the engine cranked over if the so-called self-starting button or interior switch did not succeed in stirring the car into life.

Below: The motor rally bowling along through Sandbach in the 1950s shows a very early model of car leading the way. Pioneers of motoring in the late 1890s needed the constitution of an ox to travel in such a machine, open to all that the elements could throw at the driver and his passenger. Of course, development was rapid and within a few years what had once been a novelty and a bit of fun became a real threat to the makers of horse drawn carriages and vehicles. Sandbach is well known as the original home of Foden and ERF

lorries, both companies being founded by Foden family members. Although little trace of these roots can be seen today and even the family mansion at Westfields has gone, the famous company brass band plays on. In 1887, Edwin Foden took over an established business building static industrial steam and agricultural traction engines. Foden's went into the lorry and wagon business around the turn into the 20th century. The ERF brand of diesel engined lorries was launched in the 1930s, taking the name from the initials of Edwin Richard Foden, the founder's son. The 1925 steam lorry in the photograph was one of successive generations of models that proved highly successful before the switch to diesel was made. Since 1992, Sandbach now has an annual transport festival that runs in conjunction with the National Town Criers' competition. We are not sure which event creates the greater racket!

Above: Shoppers piled on board the bus in The Square as they set off for home from the centre of Nantwich. The schoolboy on the left, waiting in line by the pillar box, was quite typically dressed for 1962. His short trousers, regulation knee length socks and cap marked out his family as traditionalists. The school satchel under his arm would have been crammed with Latin homework and geometric theorems to prove. In a year or two's time he might well notice the bobby soxed girl behind him. Then his troubles would start.

WORKING LIFE

'Take it with a pinch of salt' and 'salt of the earth' are two common expressions that we all use from time to time. However, salt was more than just part of the English language to these men. It was their source of income and they toiled hard working the brine that has been a major Cheshire industry for 2,000 years. The Romans even named Middlewich as 'Salinae', a word derived from the Latin for salt. It was so important a commodity that Roman soldiers were often paid their wages in salt; some believing that the word 'salary' is derived from this practice. None of this meant much to these men, working away in tough and sweaty conditions. Northwich, Nantwich, Middlewich and Winsford became the main centres for extraction and production. Rock salt was laid down in our region some 220 million years ago. Seawater moved inland, creating a series of shallow marshes that left deep deposits behind when the water evaporated. Both open pan working and underground mining have been used to get at the salt. Today, over half the white salt used in British cooking is produced at Middlewich.

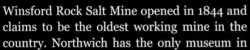

Winsford Rock Salt Mine opened in 1844 and claims to be the oldest working mine in the country. Northwich has the only museum in Britain that is dedicated to the history of salt. The story is told in the building that was once a workhouse.

Above: The canteen ladies from the Soldiers' and Sailors' Rest on Crewe Station, Nantwich Road, posed for their photograph from just after the First World War. It is not hard to determine which of these fine examples of Cheshire loveliness were the ones in charge. You did not get a hat to wear unless you were important. Nowadays, all these women would have to put on some form of head covering or the thought police from the health and safety section would have them for toast. That is toast spread with a substance containing the recommended level of polyunsaturated fat, of course. Such multisyllabic words would have sounded like so much gobbledegook to the group posing in front of the tea urns. The canteen was set up during the 1914-18 War to provide servicemen with simple refreshment as they passed through on their way to their posting. For some it might be one of their last opportunities to have good old fashioned English cuppa before transferring to a troopship taking them to the front. The ladies were well aware that a cheery word, as well as a warm drink, meant a lot to those lads. It all helped to take their minds off what might lie ahead. It was good to see a smile from someone who reminded you of a sister or sweetheart back home.

Right: The name of the Crewe County Clothing Company is something of a tongue twister, but no-one was concerned with pronunciation in December, 1943. Production was on everybody's lips instead. That was all they talked about as they worked their fingers to the bone. Christmas was just around the corner, but the question of year end bonuses was an irrelevance, even if they existed at all. The workforce was employed making uniforms for the American armed forces. The USA had finally been forced to commit itself to the war when the Japanese bombed the naval base at Pearl Harbour two years earlier. The first few divisions arrived in the UK in the late spring of 1942. They continued to arrive steadily, reaching a peak just before the Normandy landings of June 1944. As well as several million ground troops who passed through the country on their way to war theatres overseas, some two million members of the 8th US Air Force were based in this country and were extensively involved in bombing raids across the Channel. The Americans took over Burtonwood Air Base, near Warrington, in the summer of 1942. It became the largest airfield in Europe, with some 18,000 servicemen stationed there. That is a lot of chewing gum and, perhaps, even more nylons.

Above: The CWS clothing factory on Camm Street, in between Mill Street and Lord Street, is now a fitness and leisure centre, with various activities taking place inside, including martial arts and gymnastics. In 1920, it was something of a sweat shop. Row upon row of women laboured over sewing machines, churning out clothing in a process that was mind blowingly boring, but at least it filled the wage packet at the end of the week. Some of these women worked in heavy engineering and munitions factories during the war that had not long finished. They drove ambulances, buses and trams. When hostilities finished, they were expected to move aside and give the men back their traditional jobs. During and after the next war, the drudgery and boredom of factory life was relieved by the introduction of 'Workers' Playtime'. This radio variety show was broadcast three lunchtimes a week from a factory 'somewhere in Britain'. The various locations were initially secret as the government did not want to advertise the factory whereabouts to the enemy. Comedians such as Charlie Chester and Ted Ray provided the jokes and big band singers like Ann Shelton and Betty Driver the music. Until they came along, these CWS girls had to crack their own funnies and sing their own songs. Looking at the decorations, they were

probably about to launch into a couple of Christmas carols. They look to have been happy with their lot and, certainly, there were many friendships formed by the treadle pedals that would last a lifetime.

Bottom left: Arthur Moseley and George Langley were in charge of the milk delivery on Richmond Road. They posed for the cameraman in this 1940 view, with the houses at 87 and 89 behind them. Those homes are still there today, though North Ward Club, to the left, changed in appearance quite markedly over the years. The imposing old institute building was replaced by a much more mundane, squatter establishment. This fell into disrepair and became quite an eyesore in the first decade of this century. Vandals made matters worse and, in early 2010, the building was the object of a young arsonist who set fire to the club, causing several families to have to evacuate their homes for a while.

Below: Nantwich Poor Law Union was declared on 24 January, 1837, and took in no fewer that 71 local parishes, villages and towns. The guardians met fortnightly under the initial chairmanship of Reverend James Folliott. The Union House, built in 1780, was set on Beam Heath and known as Barony Workhouse. It was brought under the Poor Law umbrella and developed to accommodate 350 inmates by the end of the 19th century. The Poor Law Amendment Act of 1834 had permitted local districts to administer systems for poverty relief within their areas. It was an early form of the welfare state, though with limitations. Those in receipt of Poor Law benefits were not permitted to vote, so were denied access to the ballot box when it came to determining their future and that of the nation The Victorian gentry was good at benevolence and taking care of the less fortunate, but it was even better in retaining the whip hand and keeping the masses in their places. The workhouse was generally regarded with dread by the classes that it was built to serve. Conditions were harsh and severe. Charles Dickens in 'Oliver Twist' brought this situation to the attention of the general public. In later years, George Orwell, in 'Down and out in Paris and London', would describe workhouse life from the experience of people he met in the 1920s. Barony Workhouse was erected as a three storey red brick building in a U-shaped plan. Its bay window frontage was topped by a pediment holding a clock face. A children's home and school were added in 1880, with an infirmary catering for 70 inmates being created a decade later. The workhouse and its associated buildings were converted into Barony Hospital in 1930. It served in this capacity until 1994. After its closure it was turned into offices for the National Health Service. It is a Grade II listed building.

Nantwich Funeral Services
An Individual, Caring and Professional Service

Although 'Graham Tresidder' is the formal name of the business, over the years the well known firm of local undertakers has established itself as 'Nantwich Funeral Services'. Graham Tresidder's phenomenal reputation means that families from all over the county request the caring and sensitive skills of Graham and his team.

Now in the fourth decade since the firm was founded, its dedicated staff have served and supported thousands of bereaved families.

Graham Tresidder celebrated 33 years of providing funeral services in 2010 by making the final touches to new Nantwich Funeral Services premises at 62, Hospital Street, Nantwich. According to Graham "Our new premises provide a convenient town centre location with a relaxed atmosphere where the bereaved and their families can feel confident that all their needs and requirements will be looked after in a professional, caring and sympathetic way".

The new premises in Nantwich complement existing premises at Crewe Road, Wistaston, and in The Square, Audlem.

The present business was begun in 1977 by Fred Tresidder.

During Fred's lifetime the role of family funeral director had changed a great deal. Most family firms originated from builders and joiners with the title of 'Undertaker' simply added to their usual services.

In the early decades of the 20th century the next of kin would inform the family doctor of a death, which often

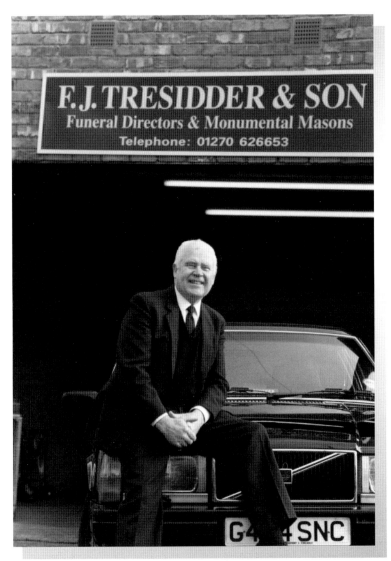

plates - which were hand painted would then be added. Should the coffin have been intended for cremation, then the interior was covered in a purple baize cloth with wooden handles and name plate. The interior of the coffin would then have several shovels full of wood shavings put into it to provide the mattress and pillow. The coffin was then lined with sheeting. This process usually took between five and eight hours to complete.

Once the coffin had been constructed the undertaker and his men would then deliver it to the house. In many cases, the doorways were too narrow to take the coffin so windows had to be removed by the undertaker's carpenter and replaced after the coffin had been taken in. Usually this was carried out in the evening or at night so as not to disturb the neighbours.

On the day of the funeral this process had to be repeated in reverse.

The front room or parlour of the deceased's home would have been chosen as the last resting place until the funeral. It was not until the late 1950s that Chapels of Rest began to be widely provided by undertakers.

By the 1970s, when Nantwich Funeral Services was established, the business of being an undertaker had evolved considerably. Undertakers were becoming 'Funeral Directors', no longer responsible just for making coffins and arranging burials, but as professionals who could take care of every aspect of dealing with the consequences of the loss of a loved one.

meant someone running to the doctor's home, or using a public telephone in the days when private telephones were rare. The same method was used, after the doctor had certified death, to call the 'layer out'. Every village and street once had such a woman.

'Last offices' were carried out by those stalwart ladies who attended to all a family's deaths - and births. The undertaker was summoned to take the necessary measurements and details. He, in turn, would call out the Clergyman or Priest to perform the 'Last Rights'. Having made the arrangements with the family, a date and time would be fixed for the funeral to take place. The undertaker would then arrange for his men to prepare and make the coffin.

In those days the coffin would then have been made from 'sets' of oak, mahogany or elm timbers. Each coffin was made to size and sealed inside with wax and bitumen. The exterior would then be sanded, sealed and polished with wax. Brass 'furniture' - handles and name

Graham followed his father Fred Tresidder, who was not only an undertaker himself and previously a

From Stage Radio T. V.

John Trent

*Top left: Founder, Fred Tresidder. **Left and above:** Fred pictured alongside company hearses outside their Nantwich premises. **Right:** A promotional card for Fred Tresidder under his stage name John Trent.*

cricket for Nantwich and Cholmondeley, league snooker, and achieved a black belt in karate.

Despite the demands of sport and work Graham managed to find time to marry his wife Christine, and to have two children Emma and David. Graham is also a member of Nantwich Rotary Club and has close links with the business community.

Very early in his career working as a funeral director Graham found himself having to take charge of the business as his father Fred was so frequently away pursuing his other interests.

cabinet-maker, but who was also a professional singer and actor.

Graham Tresidder was born in West Kirby, on Merseyside; he came to Nantwich in 1965, with his parents and sister. His father Fred Tresidder became a professional singer, but after a while opened his funeral business based as now in Hospital Street, Nantwich.

Around 1980 Graham joined his father on a full-time basis after helping out part-time for three years. When Graham left school, however, his ambition was to become a professional footballer, being on the books of Port Vale FC. When he realised he was not going to make the grade as a footballer he found a 'proper job' working for local opticians, SW & C Jackson.

However, after Graham began working in the family funeral business his father was able to expand his acting career, appearing in hundreds of television programmes and adverts.

Graham grew into the funeral business, quickly finding out how demanding but rewarding the vocation can be. The satisfaction he got from having helped a family through a traumatic time was a priceless feeling.

Though a footballing career was never to happen, Graham retains a keen interest in sport. He has played

Fred Tresidder was probably the only Funeral Director in the United Kingdom who held an Equity card, and as a result he soon started being asked to do funeral scenes in Emmerdale and Coronation Street. Through Fred's Equity card he became the regular funeral director on Coronation Street and Brookside - with his first television funeral being Ernie Bishop and his last Don Brennan the taxi driver.

Public speaking took Fred to women's institute groups, and similar speaking engagements, where he was in demand for his interesting and humorous accounts of

*Top left: Graham Tresidder. **Below:** A private and quiet room for families to make their arrangements.*

daily life as an undertaker. His popularity was immense, something which in turn increased the profile of the funeral business, which would become a well-respected and established part of the town.

Throughout his professional career Fred worked with many celebrities, and his singing has been captured on CDs, which to this day are still requested at family funerals, a remarkable testament to his memory.

Fred's acting, singing and public speaking consumed more and more of his time. As a consequence Graham soon started to take up the business in his father's absence, and his own reputation and following soon grew in the locality.

Fred retired at the age of 68 leaving Graham in full control of the firm. Since that time the business has grown significantly in size, expanding from one Nantwich location to the current three premises covering Nantwich, Audlem, and Crewe. In the course of a decade the number of funerals tripled. Graham, today working with his step-son David in the business, is still developing the services he offers in an ever-changing world.

David came into the business as a trainee and has since developed his own knowledge and understanding of the business and the needs of the firm's clients. He is now a full-time partner and funeral director. Having been brought up in the environment all his life he has easily stepped into the role, as his step-father Graham did over three decades earlier when he too followed his father into the business.

According to Graham Tresidder "I think there is a special bond within any family business, but especially so in our particular work; it is not something you can easily train for, you have to have the personality and ability to be sympathetic and caring, understanding, and able

Above: Advertising literature. *Below:* Third generation David (left) and Graham.

to at all times keep your own counsel, always putting the needs of the bereaved first, even in very difficult and demanding circumstances".

Staff at Nantwich Funeral Services have over 75 years of collective experience and, with great care and understanding, continuously help and guide families through difficult times in their lives. Working in this environment means all staff have to be compassionate, caring and dedicated, everyone in the team has to work well together to minimise stress for families; often the job places exceptional demands on staff both physically and emotionally, so being able to rely on each other is vital to enable families to receive the highest standard of professional expertise and care. The team at Nantwich Funeral Services all work closely together. "Being able to rely on your colleagues for help and support is vital," says Graham. "We have both a pleasant and caring environment and have a fantastic team, each member of which is immensely valued for their contribution."

Most clients are from a ten mile radius of the firm's offices; however, the firm also organises many funerals much further afield at the request of families. It is not unusual for Graham and his staff to be asked to direct a funeral in other counties at the request of a family who have moved away.

The majority of Funeral Directors obtain business through recommendation and referral. Nantwich Funeral Services is no exception, with a long-standing relationship and excellent reputation within the community for providing a caring and quality service. Families trust the firm and come back again and again when the need arises. Those relationships are based on trust and professionalism, and it is these key attributes which have enabled the firm to thrive.

The fact that families come back repeatedly when they need such services, the number of funerals conducted, and that the firm now has three locations within the borough means that most families' requirements can be met. Attention to detail and the dedication of the team plays an important part in the firm's success.

Sometimes there are unusual requests: many families are now looking for a 'funeral with a difference'. Graham and his team can always fulfil a family's wishes, and offer an extensive range of products and services to accommodate these. That 'special touch' to a funeral is important, and if, say, that means providing an unusual type of coffin then they can do that too.

A funeral is the last opportunity for a spouse or family member to remember their loved one; there is only get one chance to get it right. Graham recognises this each and every time he is asked to arrange a funeral and strives to ensure that every last detail is always taken of.

According to Graham: "We help to make sure that every funeral we arrange is made as special as the person who has died, each and every funeral is a unique celebration of that person's life. Today, families expect attention to detail and we make sure that we can cater for their every need; for example, we are able to provide an extensive range of funeral vehicles, ranging from the usual limousines through to motorbikes and horse drawn carriages."

As a family-run business Nantwich Funeral Services prides itself on being able to give a dedicated 24-hour personal service. When a bereaved family member wants to speak to their funeral director they need to be assured that they will be there immediately, they don't want to be sent through to a call centre, and a familiar voice at the end of the phone is a real comfort.

As Graham explains: "We aim to provide all families with a professional and dignified service at all times and our experience and reputation enables us to do this. We are pleased to be able to help families in their time of grief and endeavour to make this period of their lives as free of difficulty as it can it possibly be."

Since conducting its first funeral in the 1970s Nantwich Funeral Services has earned a well-deserved reputation within the community for providing a caring and quality service, with all the skill and experience necessary to look after bereaved families in their moment of need. This is how the company continues to be a success; it has become a part of the local community, where families trust the help and support they receive.

Sadly, in 2007 Fred Tresidder passed away after a long illness, but his memory still lives on through his son Graham, grandson David - and the business he founded.

*Top left, bottom left and above: The firm's premises at 448 Crewe Road, Wistaston (top left), The Square, Audlem (bottom left) and 62 Hospital Street, Nantwich (above). **Below:** The firm caters for all needs, an example being the motorbike service seen here.*

British Salt - Two Thousand Years of History

From its manufacturing plant at Middlewich, British Salt Limited supplies around half the United Kingdom's total demand for domestic and industrial salt. The plant is able to produce more than 800,000 tonnes of salt a year, supplying the food, chemical, water-treatment, hide and skin, and other industries, and also supplying clean, white salt for de-icing during the winter. The company is a key employer in the Crewe area and is now the only remaining salt works in Middlewich.

Salt was probably being produced from Cheshire brine as long ago as the Iron Age when early Britons first found a brine spring.

The Romans produced salt at Middlewich by evaporation of brine in large vessels. Following the Roman invasion of Britain Middlewich was named Salinae because of the salt deposits around it. It became one of their major sites for salt production.

During this time the Romans built a fort at Harbutts Field, to the north of the town, where recent excavations to the south of the fort have found evidence of further Roman activity, including a well and part of a preserved Roman road.

The 11th century Domesday Book suggests that the salt making area existed as a separate industrial enclave between the surrounding urban settlements of Kinderton and Newton. Unlike the Domesday entry for Nantwich, where the 'wich' is enclosed within a boundary ditch, there is no suggestion in the Middlewich entry that the Middle 'wich' enclave was contained within a similar enclosure.

By around the 13th century, the settlement of Middlewich had grown to contain about a hundred or so six-lead 'wich houses'. These were tightly packed together along narrow streets around the town's two brine pits. The middle 'wich' itself occupied land on both sides of the River Croco. Middlewich deeds before 1450 refer more to four and eight-lead wich houses than to six-lead wich houses, but after 1450 the six-lead wich house appears to have become the standard. The same situation appears to have existed at Nantwich.

This page: *Images of early open pan lump salt production.*

straightened, a channel being constructed for it alongside the canal (which then became the boundary between the townships of Kinderton and Newton, with the ancient course of the River Croco remaining as the boundary line between the townships of Middlewich and Kinderton).

Meanwhile the 'Open Pan' method of salt production continued right to the middle of the 20th Century, after which 'multiple-effect' evaporation technology was introduced.

In 1917, Staveley Coal and Iron Company Limited bought land in Sandbach on which to

Camden's 'Magna Brittania' written in 1580 reports that 'From thence runneth Wever down by Nantwich, not far from Middlewich, and so to Northwich. These are very famous Salt-Wiches, five or six miles distant, where brine or salt water is drawn out of pits, which they pour not upon wood while it burneth as the ancient Gauls and Germans were wont to do, but boil it over a fire to make salt thereof. Neither doubt I that these were known unto the Romans, and that from hence was usually paid the Custom of Salt, called Salarium.' The modern word 'salary' of course comes directly from the ancient custom of making payments in salt rather than in cash.

Somewhat earlier, a record of the number of Middlewich salt houses in 1507 includes a list of payments by occupiers of wich houses. This gives a total of 110 wich houses of six-leads. This figure compares with the 216 wich houses of six-leads recorded for Nantwich in a 1624 survey.

A large portion of what was 'walling land' connected with the wich houses is today covered by the Trent and Mersey Canal, which in 1775 cut a broad swathe through the centre of the area once covered with medieval wich houses – though in fact they had gone long before the canal was built. The once narrow and winding bed of the River Croco was at the same time

build a salt works. Construction began around 1920, the salt produced being a feedstock for a new brine electrolysis plant in Chesterfield. This electrolysis plant produced caustic soda and chlorine for a rapidly expanding chemical industry.

In 1960, Staveley increased its salt interests through the purchase of the production facilities of Palmer Mann Limited, of Elworth, Sandbach. That company had just been acquired by Cerebos Limited, so that it gained the Sifta Salt brand. Cerebos retained the brand names whilst Staveley concentrated on bulk salt production.

In 1967, a new company, British Salt Limited, was created to manage the salt production interests of Cerebos and Staveley. Staveley owned 75% of the new business and Cerebos the remaining 25%.

Top and above right: *Early bulk salt delivery tankers.* **Left:** *Well head at Warmingham Brinefield.*

The expansion raised the production capacity from 600,000 tonnes a year to its current 840,000 tonnes per annum.

Following nationalisation of the Coal and Steel industries, The Staveley Coal and Iron Company restructured itself. The new Staveley Industries now concentrated on manufacturing, mechanical and electrical services, weighing and measurement, and of course salt. In 1982, Staveley acquired the entire share capital of British Salt Limited.

British Salt has a licence to abstract water from a local river, which is matched to the plants maximum capacity. The licence essentially permits water to be 'borrowed' from the river, which is returned (after having been distilled out of the brine) to another brook, in an extremely pure form.

A modern, new, highly-efficient, salt manufacturing plant of 600,000 tonne capacity was built at Middlewich alongside the Cerebos facility. The commercial arrangements were such that Staveley would be the sole producer of pure white salt, whilst Cerebos would concentrate on packaging for the retail sector.

The amount of water extracted is therefore a small proportion of the total water requirement, as much of the condensed water is now returned to the brinefield to be re-circulated. Since the controlled brine pumping was started over 20 years ago, the stream has never approached a dry state despite droughts and imposed restrictions.

The new plant started production in 1969, leading to the closure of two old Cerebos plants, and the closure of the British Soda plant and the Palmer Mann plant in Sandbach. A conveyor carried salt directly from the British Salt plant to the Cerebos packaging plant.

*Top left: The official opening of British Salt by HRH Prince Philip on 25 June, 1969. **Left:** Part of the present British Salt fleet. **Below:** Views inside the undried salt storage warehouse.*

In 1973, the Middlewich plant capacity was increased and became the first '6-effect' plant in the world. Purified brine is fed into the evaporating plant to drive off water and deposit salt crystals out of solution. The resulting salt slurry is passed through each evaporation vessel in series, the brine boiling at ever decreasing pressure and temperature. Just one input of steam is required to generate the heat for this energy intensive process. This advanced evaporator design ensures maximum utilisation and conservation of energy.

In June 2007, the British Salt Management Team, backed by Lloyds Development Capital, led a buyout of the business from its American owners. Thus, the ownership of this traditional British business came back where it belongs, in the United Kingdom.

Today the Management Team is committed to ensuring that British Salt remains the primary white salt producer in the UK. Investment continues with renewal of the cross-country mains that bring the brine into Middlewich from Warmingham. Meanwhile, gas storage will continue to be a very important part of the business in the future.

Salt producers over the years have tapped into underground streams, having the effect of creating subsidence of the land above. However, on the brinefield located at Warmingham British Salt uses the method of 'controlled brine pumping'. Water is forced underground to dissolve the salt and cavities are developed to a controlled shape and size, thus preventing subsidence.

The development of these stable, tight underground cavities since the mid-1970s has provided British Salt with another business opportunity. The nature of these cavities makes them ideal for storing Natural Gas. This is a much safer way of storing gas than in an above-ground gasometer. British Salt has sold ten cavities to EDF Energy and has also developed another four cavities for EDF Trading.

In 2000, Staveley Industries sold the British Salt business to an American consortium, US Salt LLC. The new millennium was a difficult time for the salt industry, with many traditional salt-using industries, such as textiles and dyeing, moving abroad. There was some consolidation in the industry when British Salt acquired the New Cheshire Salt Works, of Northwich. With expensive energy costs, the smaller less-efficient NCSW plant was closed down and all production moved to Middlewich.

Top left and above: Aerial view of the British Salt site. Below: Rob Jones (left), after 40 years service, handing over the CEO role to Bill Thompson (right) in July 2010.

Flowcrete - For The World At Your Feet

April 2010 witnessed the official opening of Flowcrete's new offices at Sandbach by HRH The Duke of Gloucester. Based at Booth Lane, Sandbach, Flowcrete UK Ltd is today just one arm of a globally important group of companies. Over the course of just three decades it has grown from one man and his daughter into a worldwide multi-million pound enterprise.

The company is the world's leading specialist flooring company with manufacturing plants across Europe, the Americas, Asia and Africa, a global commercial and sales support team and the backing of a major multi-national manufacturing group. Flowcrete provides the same high standard of product and service across the globe."

Manufacturing a wide-range of products that fulfil every flooring requirement, the firm's products include Flowfast - fast-track installation flooring, Flowfresh - antimicrobial polyurethane flooring, Deckshield -

waterproof car park decking, Isocrete K-Screed - fast-drying floor screed, Mondéco - seamless resin terrazzo, Isowarm - underfloor heating, Rustik - stone carpets, Corrosion Protection, Antistatic Coatings, colourful and contemporary Commercial Flooring systems as well as a number of specialist Industrial Flooring systems and Surface Treatments.

Research and development laboratories are constantly innovating new products and improving existing ones to ensure that clients benefit from the best in modern flooring technology. The company is committed to pioneering greener flooring products that adhere to a policy of environmental protection as well as introducing automated installation methods that keep Flowcrete at the forefront of the industry.

An international client base includes NASA, Lufthansa, BAA, Nestlé, Kraft, Coca-Cola, AstraZeneca, GlaxoSmithKline, Jaguar, Bentley, BP, LG and Sony as well as Wembley Stadium, O2 Arena and Dubai, Kuala Lumpur and Hong Kong International Airports.

But how did such a remarkable business grow from tiny beginnings?

One fine day in 1982 a man from Mars (Mars Confectionery in fact) challenged British inventor, Peter Gibbins, to develop a special type of flooring that would stop sugar eating into the floors in his production plant. Peter was about to sell the man from Mars his ingenious formulation, when his

Top left: Founder, Peter Gibbins demonstrates Flowcrete products to Lady Ann Winterton in 1968. Above: Flowcrete's new sustainable offices. Left: The sales team pictured in 1989.

wife finally cracked, saying, "for goodness sake, why don't you just set up in business?"

With the help of his ambitious daughter, Dawn Gibbins, Peter created Flowcrete that same year, starting out in a small manufacturing unit located in the heart of Cheshire. David Greaves joined the business as a partner and over the following years Peter, David and Dawn worked round the clock to build solid foundations for the company and guarantee its long-term future in a competitive marketplace.

In 1984 Flowcrete secured their first major project for NATO, where their infra-red reflective coatings went down a treat. Their success was further cemented a few years later when they were awarded their first Department of Trade and Industry Award for Innovation. By 1989 Flowcrete's turnover had reached £500,000 of materials and was poised to grow further – this coincided with the arrival of Mark Greaves – a dynamic entrepreneur fresh out of business school, Mark, who was married to Dawn, was to go on to lead the company and still remains at the helm of business operations today.

Mark recalls how diplomatic he had to be at times working in an office with his wife, his father and his father-in-law.

During the early nineties Flowcrete continued to go from strength to strength launching its polyurethane flooring systems to the food and drinks industry, promoting its waterproof car park deck coatings, developing its water-based flooring technologies and securing a patent for its deep penetrating hardening system, which was proving to be a revolution in sub-floor repair. In 1994, Dawn became the youngest ever industrialist to receive an MBE, for services to industry, but was heartbroken that Peter was unable to witness her success following his death from cancer the previous year.

Along the way, Dawn had also won the Veuve Clicquot Businesswoman of the Year Award and been recognised by Her Majesty the Queen as a Pioneer for the Life of Our Nation.

*Top: The Flowcrete team, 1989. **Left:** Flowcrete's technical team, 1994. **Below:** Dawn Gibbins receives her MBE for Services to Industry.*

Though Dawn's MBE was awarded for services to industry her staff and clients felt it should stand for her key attribute of – "Making Business Enjoyable".

Mark Greaves joined Flowcrete in 1989 after four years with Shell International, where he was Business Manager for its UK retail lubricants business - a role in which he doubled profits in three years. He went to Shell from Manchester Business School (MBS). At Manchester, Mark achieved an MBA with Distinction and was the highest performing candidate of his graduating year in 1986. Prior to attending MBS, Mark was a student at Bristol University, where he achieved a degree in English Literature.

Since joining the company in 1989, Mark has taken the business from its Cheshire roots and established it as a major global player within the industry, leading to its current position with sales offices in 29 countries and eight manufacturing centres, spanning four continents worldwide.

The measure of his successful contribution to global expansion is best reflected in financial terms. Back in 1989 Flowcrete's turnover stood at £0.5 million - against a figure twenty years later of £55 million. Mark has engineered two large scale international acquisition deals, giving Flowcrete the necessary infrastructure to grow and continue to develop, with the purchase of Swedish-based Perstorp Construction Chemicals in 2002 and South Africa's Ivory Industrials in 2006.

It was back in 1995, however, that Flowcrete's march to world domination really began with the acquisitions of Isocrete Floor Screeds, Gyvlon Floor Screeds, Chryso UK and Beaver Anchorlyte. At the same time as buying companies in the UK, Flowcrete was stretching out, opening offices in Hong Kong, Singapore, Thailand, China and a manufacturing plant in Kuala Lumpur, Malaysia. In this period of fast growth a number of projects were coming online, including the largest ever screed contract to date at Chek Lap Kok Airport, in Hong Kong, as well as high-profile installations at the Millennium Stadium, in Cardiff, and the iconic Millennium Dome, in London.

At the turn of the millennium, Flowcrete opened a new commercial sales office in the UAE and entered into a

joint venture in Brazil with a local company to penetrate the South American market. New flooring innovations included Isowarm - underfloor heating as well as a range of seamless antimicrobial systems capable of destroying bacteria at ground-level.

With an ever-growing client-base including Kuala Lumpur International Airport, in Malaysia, Nokia, GlaxoSmithKline, Roche

Top left: Mark Greaves, Robert Street and Tony Ford negotiating acquitition of Isocrete in 1995. *Centre:* A selection of Flowcrete installations: Soccer City, South Africa (top left) Bentley Motors UK (bottom left), NASA (top right), Wembley (centre right) and Manchester Airport (bottom right). *Below:* Flowcrete receive Investor in People Standard in 2007.

Today, Flowcrete is recognised as a truly international company. It spans the globe with commercial sales offices and manufacturing plants worldwide. In 2008, Flowcrete became part of Ohio-based RPM International Inc, a $35bn New York stock-exchange listed company with subsidiaries that manufacture and market high-performance coatings, sealants and speciality chemicals. In 2009, Flowcrete was rewarded for its international success in exporting British flooring technology overseas in the form of a Queen's Award for Enterprise, which it achieved in the category of International Trade.

Pharmaceuticals, L'Oréal and Sharjah Mega Mall Shopping Centre in the Middle East, the world really did seem to be at Flowcrete's feet - and with the further acquisitions of Atako Corrosion Protection and Perstorp Construction Chemicals in 2002 Flowcrete had much to celebrate on its 20th birthday.

Committed to engineering the perfect flooring solution every time, Flowcrete is a unique success story, with an interesting and exciting family-based history. With a bright future ahead one thing is clear, the Flowcrete story has many more chapters yet to be written.

Top left: *The Flowcrete Team celebrate winning the Queens Award for Enterprise, 2009.* *Above, left and below:* *Mark Greaves (left) and HRH Duke of Gloucester at the official opening of Flowcrete's new Sandbach office, pictured left and below, 2010.*

The following years saw Flowcrete enter the South African, Australian and North American markets, as well as strengthening its presence on the European Continent and throughout the Asia-Pacific rim. The launch of its Flowfast system in 2006 generated further success as the flooring innovation - capable of curing in just 2 hours - raced across the globe. Another triumph came in securing Flowcrete's biggest contract to date - an £8m project at the exclusive Jumeirah Lakes Towers development in the Middle East.

Poole Alcock LLP - Going to Law

The prominent firm of solicitors, Poole Alcock LLP, today with offices not only in Crewe but in no fewer than nine locations altogether, is one of the longest-established legal firms in the region.

Founder of the firm was Francis Joseph Poole. Born in 1867, he was the third son of Mark Poole, a Boot and Shoe Manufacturer in Sandbach.

Francis Joseph trained as a solicitor, which then involved five years as an articled clerk, and a fee of £80 – in those days a large sum. Francis was initially articled to a solicitor of Oldham. However, this was not satisfactory as the practice comprised, for most part, small debt collecting. Francis Joseph was re-articled to a firm in London, and half the £80 fee returned.

Francis Joseph Poole began his own practice in a one-room office in Widnes. An office was also opened in Sandbach.

A younger brother, Charles, born in 1877, also qualified as a solicitor and the two set up in partnership.

Francis Poole married Hannah Foden in 1895. Hannah was the daughter of Edwin Foden, founder of the rapidly growing firm of steam-wagon makers Edwin Foden & Sons. Francis Joseph was at one time Chairman of the Directors of Foden's Limited, and Pooles were, of course, the solicitors for 'Fodens'.

Francis and Hannah had only one child, a son Francis 'Frank' Foden Poole, born in 1902.

In 1926 Elworth Cricket Club was looking for new premises and as Captain of the team, Frank approached his parents who

donated land to the rear of Boothville, their family home, to the club. In 1937, jointly with a Mr and Mrs Alec Palmer, they gifted Elworth Park to the town.

Francis Joseph was a leading member of the United Methodist Free Church. He served on the Cheshire County Council, became an Alderman, and was a Governor at Sandbach School. One of his main interests was improving Elworth. The preservation of trees and wide road at Park Lane, Abbey Road and Middlewich Road are a result.

Francis Joseph Poole died in 1937, his wife Hannah in 1948. Their son Frank Poole died in 1979.

Meanwhile Thomas Jones Alcock was born in 1882 in Everton, Liverpool, the birthplace of his mother Sara. In the 1890s the family were living in Congleton where his father, William, was a pawnbroker.

By 1901 Thomas, aged 18 years old, was a Solicitors Clerk and was Articled locally.

With the start of the Great War in 1914 Thomas joined the Royal Engineers and fought in France and Italy.

Thomas later married Minnie Charlesworth. They lived in Crewe Road, Sandbach. They had two sons (William) Arnold born in 1923 and Ronald Thomas born in 1925, both of whom joined the practice. Arnold stayed with the company as a clerk, whilst Ronald did not stay and took up managing a farm instead.

Thomas's nephew, John Alcock, was born in 1928. After completing National Service he joined the firm as a Legal Executive, working there until the mid-1990s.

Thomas J Alcock was the Chairman of the local Law Society and also a Lay Minister of the Methodist Church. He continued working until his death in 1963, aged 81. His wife Minnie had died in 1957.

(William) Arnold Alcock died in 1998 aged 75, Ronald Thomas Alcock in 2007 aged 82. John Alcock died in 2008 at the age of 80.

Harold Charlesworth, Minnie's nephew, was Senior Partner throughout the 1960s, followed by David Ellis Harrison in the 1970s and 80s.

Poole Alcock became one of the leading firms of solicitors in south Cheshire with the merger of five solicitor practices: Herbert Wilkinson, of Middlewich, Frederick Cook & Son, of Crewe, Clive Smith, of Nantwich, Davies & Co, of Alsager, and Timperley & Co, of Crewe, Alsager and Nantwich.

Poole Alcock LLP today provides clients with a valued local service. Friendly, caring, professional staff work alongside partners Michael Bracegirdle, Senior Partner since 1999, Geoff Goodwin, Dianne Mooney, Charles Smalley, Phillip Harrison, David Gaut, Sarah Jarrett, Andrew Roberts and Scott Harding. There are now offices in Alsager, Chester, Congleton, Nantwich, Northwich, Warrington, Sandbach and Crewe.

Top left: *An early Poole family photograph. Pictured are founder Francis Joseph (back left), his wife Hannah (centre), Edward (front left) and Charles (front right).* **Left:** *The Alcock family pictured in the early 20th century. Back row L-R: Thomas J, William, and Samuel, front seated is James.* ***Above:*** *Poole Alcock's Middlewich Road, Sandbach, premises.*

Malbank School & Sixth Form College
Centuries of Learning

Located in Welsh Row, Nantwich, Malbank School today is an 11-18 school serving the needs of over 1,300 pupils and Sixth Form students.

Formerly the Nantwich and Acton Grammar School, Malbank is proud of both its past and present - and is looking forward to an even brighter future. Its story began with the Nantwich Grammar School, founded in 1560. That school stood on the Northwest corner of the churchyard, at the geographical heart of Nantwich.

The Grammar School was founded by woolpackers from London: their family name of Thrush is still used today as a House name. The first recorded Headmaster was Randal Kent (1572-1623). He obviously felt a great affection for the school because a porch was added which had the following inscription in Latin: 'Randal Kent, high master of this school, out of his unique love for good learning and his extreme affection for this native place, at his own expense enlarged this the very seat of the new Muses, with this new addition'

The school was fortunate to escape the Great Fire of Nantwich in 1583. A few years later in 1617 King James I visited Nantwich and attended a service at the church where he heard an oration in Latin from one of the scholars of the school.

Malbank continues to be proud of its links with the history of the town. In 1642 the battle of Nantwich took place during the English Civil War. Brererton, the commander of the parliamentary forces in the battle, is used as a House name today. A cannon ball from the conflict was found on school land in the 1930s and can still be seen today in the Headteacher's office.

Through out the 18th and 19th century Latin grammar continued to be a central element of education. An ex-pupil, William Walford, noted in the 1780s the 'daily drudgery' that this involved. By 1860, however, the school had moved to Welsh Rowe. At this point Nantwich Grammar School amalgamated with the Blue Cap Charity School which had been founded in 1712.

All Boys residing in the parish of Nantwich, 'of the age of five years or upwards' were allowed to attend, but were not allowed to stay at the school after reaching sixteen.

By then the curriculum had widened to include subjects that would be recognisable today, such as History, Geography, French and English Literature. Teaching methods, however,

*Top: The porch which was added to the school by the first recorded Headmaster, Randal Kent. **Left:** An early view of Nantwich Grammar. **Above:** A school photo from 1875, a time when only boys were permitted to attend.*

The Grammar School era ended in 1977 when the school became comprehensive and changed its name to Malbank.

Whilst Malbank treasures its past, it has an innovative culture which focuses on preparing its students for the future. As the representative Olympic School for Cheshire, it places strong emphasis on the Olympic and Paralympic values. Student Leadership programmes are at the heart of its child-centred culture.

were very different from today. A pupil who left in 1885 recalled that the headmaster, Mr Hirst, used to 'emphasis his teaching by the application of the stick, but his sticks were usually branches from current bushes from the garden and they did not hurt much.'

In 1885 the grammar school at Acton closed and amalgamated with Nantwich Grammar School. Nantwich and Acton Grammar School (NAGS) is still recalled through the presences of two horses' heads on the Malbank School coat of arms.

After 350 years of teaching only boys the school continued to grow with the decision taken in 1905 to admit girls for the first time. By 1913 a new school building was started but work halted because of the outbreak of the First World War. Completion of the new premises in 1921 led to the relocation of the school to its present position on Welsh Rowe.

The school celebrated its 450th anniversary with a full school ceremony and visit from the Duke of Gloucester on 26 April, 2010.

Today, the school celebrates its historic legacy, but more than four centuries after its founding it equally looks to the future, aiming to produce young people who will leave the school to make positive contributions locally, nationally and internationally in the long years still ahead.

Top left: A 1905 school photograph at which time girls were attending. ***Above:*** *The girls hockey team, 1909/10.* ***Below:*** *Malbank School, 2010.*

Jaymar - Packaging Progress

Jaymar Packaging Limited is a privately owned, family-run company specialising in the manufacture of a wide range of customised cartons and cartonboard packaging.

Company founders Bill Street and Stan Baker first met in 1977. Bill was a shift supervisor at McCorquodales, the cheque printing company in Crewe; Stan was a sales representative for Pinnacle Packaging, in Leek.

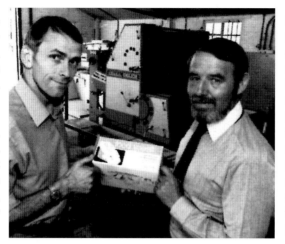

They decided to set up a carton producing company using their life savings, and their homes as collateral. The name was intended to be 'Kaymar Packaging' a mixture of their wives' names, Kay and Marie, but the name already existed, so J was substituted for K.

Premises were rented near Nantwich. Two ancient Heidelberg machines were bought - one for printing and the other for cutting out. With a guillotine and an old van, Bill and Stan were ready for business. The products were mainly for the leather goods, hardware, mail-order sectors and credit card voucher boxes which required either plain, or very simply printed cartons.

Bill and Stan were soon approached by a retired gentleman who wanted some part-time work. Ted Sharman was extremely hard working; one of his main duties, other than to make tea in a massive brown teapot, was to bail the waste and stack it for recycling. This was mechanised in later years, and a vending machine installed, but Ted stayed with the company doing odd jobs until ill-health forced his retirement in 1994 at the age of 89.

Once the products were printed and cut out they had to be glued - some would be taken to a gluing company in Manchester and some taken by Kay to outworkers on her way home to be collected the following morning. Kay also kept the ledger of orders and typed delivery notes and invoices until 1987 when there was sufficient administration to justify employing someone in the office full-time: this was Eileen Mason, still with the company today.

There was no forklift truck in the early years so deliveries had to be loaded and unloaded by hand. The building was very cold; when a straight-line 'gluer' was bought to save the cost of sending work out, both Kay and Marie ran the machine wearing overcoats. In 1983 an apprentice was employed, followed by two more in 1985. All those former YTS staff are still employed in key jobs.

As orders increased the company moved to a larger, but no more comfortable, unit on the same estate and purchased another cylinder machine.

In 1984, however, Bill and Stan realised that the market for their products was shrinking. Multi-colour work was appearing even on the least expensive products. In response a brand new two-colour lithographic press was acquired.

At this time, Marie Baker gave Stan a micro computer for Christmas. Stan wrote a program which could produce quotations. This was developed by a software house into an integrated package which would cover stock control. This gave the company a critical lead over its competitors.

Top: Founders, Bill Street (left) and Stan Baker with the new Roland Parva machine in 1984. Left: Jaymar's second site at Wardle. Above: A Heidelberg Cylinder machine, the same as the machines the company started with.

It was a considerable honour to be a finalist and demonstrate how far the company's production facilities had come.

When the company was formed there were many small carton producers; most of them are no longer trading. The cost of investing in plant, computerised systems and quality accreditation was enormous but necessary to continue to meet the demands of an ever-changing market.

In 1988 the firm moved to its current premises in First Avenue, Crewe Gates Industrial Estate. Ironically, the former owners were McCorquodales. The building could easily accommodate an additional five-colour press. This allowed Jaymar to produce more complex packaging and longer print-runs. By 1995 the original 27,500 square feet was increased to 32,500. The company now took on two sales executives, an internal sales co-ordinator, a designer and a plate-maker.

Marie Baker passed away in 1999 and Stan decided to retire. As Bill and Kay's son, Craig, had by now joined the company, the Street family bought Stan's shares.

Gary Marsh was appointed Production Director in 2005, and with Director Craig Street, a new management team was formed.

Jaymar employs thirty staff and is proud of their loyalty and dedication; over half have 20 years or more service, helping to maintain a family atmosphere. Bill and Kay now take a less active role in the day-to-day running of the business; the management team, however, continues to concentrate on their principles of controlled growth, investment, service and quality.

Fresh investment has been made to increase capacity and efficiency. One customer was so delighted with the printing of a new carton that they asked Jaymar to enter the product in the prestigious PrintWeek packaging awards competition.

Top left: Kay counting and packing cartons on the first gluing machine in 1980. *Above left:* The 5 colour plus coater Roland 700 press the company now runs. *Top right:* Kay and Bill Street, 2010. *Below:* Jaymar's First Avenue, Crewe Gates Industrial Estate, premises.

F J Need - Fine Food Since 1973

F J Need (Foods) Limited is a family run business established in 1973 by the late John Need. It is currently run by his son and daughter Paul and Tracey Need. After 21 years of expansion and upgrading, the company moved to Spinneyfields Farm, in the heart of dairy land in Worleston, on the outskirts of Nantwich - the name taken from the firm's well-known brand of selected cheese.

Behind its rural appearance Spinneyfields Farm hides some of the latest technology with a purpose-built state of the art grating line. The range of grated and diced products has been specially formulated for the pizza, manufacturing, catering and wholesale markets.

John Need moved to Crewe from Essex in the late 1950s. In Crewe he helped run his father's fish and chip shop and fish round. In 1962 he married his wife Sandra Bayley.

After taking various jobs to support his family, by 1973 John was working as a driver for Holland's Cheese based at Calveley Mill, Tarporley. His ambition, however, was to work for himself, and during a two week holiday he experimentally bought cheese from wholesalers, cut it up and sold it himself to corner shops. As a result John soon handed in his notice at Holland's.

Working from home in Coleridge Way in Crewe, John bought in 40lb blocks of cheese and, together with his family, cut them into smaller blocks and delivered them to local shops in a small white refrigerated van.

John's neighbours, however, were not too pleased that a cheese business was being run from residential premises, and so the fledgling firm soon moved, first to a store by Cumberland Bridge and, in 1976, to Gresty Road, Crewe.

Seven years later, John sold his firm to the Albert Fisher Group plc though he remained as managing director. In the following year, 1984, he bought Holland's Cheese, the business he had left in 1973, and moved back into Calveley Mill once more. Employee status, however, no longer suited John and, in 1986, he bought the company back.

Top left: Founder, John Need. *Below left:* Spinneyfields Farm. *Top right:* F J Need's second company vehicle. *Above:* Holland's Cheese the company John Need worked for and then purchased in 1984.

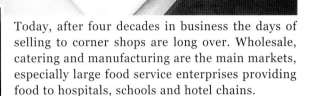

A year later John bought Bank House Farm on Crewe Road, Wistaston. He converted the outbuildings to a home and used the original main house as offices. Production was run from a warehouse on Huntsbank Industrial Park.

With further expansion soon needed Mile End Farm, at Worleston, was bought. Outbuildings were converted into offices and a purpose-built warehouse constructed in which a modern grating line was soon installed. The farm would be renamed Spinneyfields Farm after the firm's now well-established brand name.

Nor was that to be John's only business enterprise: in 1995 John Need founded a second business, The Salt Company Ltd, which is run from the same premises as FJ Need (Foods) Ltd.

Paul Seddon joined the company in 1975 as an accountant and is now Financial Director.

Company founder John Need passed away in 2000 at the young age of 57. Today, the business is owned by Sandra Need and is run by her son and daughter, Paul and Tracey.

Paul Need joined the company at the age of 16; today he is Managing Director. Tracey Need worked in the company office before taking time off to start a family of her own: she rejoined the company in 1992 and is now a Director.

John Need's grandchildren, James, Charlotte, Matthew and Chloe, have all worked in the business and, who knows, may yet make it a career choice themselves.

Today, after four decades in business the days of selling to corner shops are long over. Wholesale, catering and manufacturing are the main markets, especially large food service enterprises providing food to hospitals, schools and hotel chains.

Nor is cheese sold much in blocks. Though the business began life with block cheese, today, due to changes in demand, the bulk of business is grated cheese, though cheese is still sold in block form. Cheese, however is not the firm's only product – the Spinneyfield brand is branching out, with the recent launch of Spinneyfield sauces.

Thanks to John Need, 'FJ' to his employees, the business he founded in 1973 has grown remarkably. From tiny beginnings today the company's annual turnover is now £32 million. That's an awful lot of cheese.

Top left: Quality control. *Top right:* Packaging Spinneyfields Block Cheese. *Top inset:* Spinneyfields cheese varieties. *Above:* A selection of Spinneyfields sauces and mayonnaises. *Below:* One of the Spinneyfields fleet.

Barratt's Coaches - Onwards and Upwards

Coach trips provide some of the happiest memories we are ever likely to have.

Some older folk still refer to coaches as 'charas', short for charabanc the very first motorised version of wooden-seated open-topped horse drawn vehicles once used by tourists.

Today's 'charas' are a far cry from those early vehicles, many with air conditioning, toilets and catering facilities. And no wooden seats.

The best privately owned coaching business in the area is the well known firm of Barratt's Coaches Ltd, now based in Sandbach.

The firm was founded by Walter Johnson Barratt. After being demobbed from the forces in 1946 he returned home to work at Harvey's tanners.

Walter, however, soon went into partnership with Maurice Maggs a local taxi operator, plus a sleeping partner from Winsford.

In those early austere post-war days it was difficult to build a business: the fledgling firm had only one elderly vehicle, a 'Dennis Big Four' 33-seater.

Since a garage would have been too expensive the coach was kept at the rear of the Red Lion pub in Nantwich.

There was little work, largely just day trips to Blackpool, Chester Zoo, Rhyl and Llandudno. Some other small, badly paid jobs, however, were also obtained from the County Council at various schools.

It was hard work just finding and retaining business, alongside keeping the coach clean as well as repairing a vehicle for which there was barely enough money to buy spare parts.

Eventually more work began to come in and Walter decided that a better coach was needed. A Foden 33-seater was quite an improvement on the old Dennis – but the cost was high, £12,000, a purchase price which would have taken every penny the partners possessed.

However, Walter's partners refused to put any more money into the enterprise whose financial outlook to them seemed precarious. Walter was forced to pay off his partners and struggle on alone.

Top left: Founder, Walter Barratt. ***Below left:*** *Dorée and Walter pictured in 1942.* ***Below:*** *Trippers take time to pose for the camera, 1954.* ***Above:*** *Walter and daughter Gillian, today's Managing Director.*

Things did begin to improve when more work was obtained. Walter worked regular shifts, sometimes working all night and very often working all the following day too - harming his health into the bargain as he and his wife struggled to buy more coaches on the back of the tiny firm's increasing reputation for reliability.

Walter Barratt was tremendously fortunate in his choice of wife. Walter and his wife Dorée had a daughter, Gillian, in 1957.

That same year Dorée obtained a Passenger Service Vehicle licence of her own. She began driving coaches with baby Gillian in a carry cot perched on top of the engine cover – fast asleep when the engine was running, wide a wake when it stopped.

The firm bought its first brand new coach in 1965, gradually improving both its fleet and its service over the following years.

Sadly, Walter died in 1973 after a long illness. Despite the loss of Walter his wife Dorée was determined to keep the business going. She had one extra driver working for her and used part-time drivers wherever she could find them.

Gillian Barratt joined the business in 1979 after attending college to study Business and Languages – a course of study which enabled the firm to begin continental work. The first foreign trip was a Paris Weekend, for the ladies from a local fishing club.

Onwards and upwards was Dorée's motto – the firm was in due course running no fewer than 18 coaches, seven of them the 'continental' type with on-board toilets and catering facilities. The once tiny one-coach business had become the largest private coach operator in South Cheshire.

Dorée drove coaches herself until she was 81 years old, having driven all over England and to the continent. Dorée retired in 2006 handing all the reins over to Gillian who had in fact been effectively in charge since 1984.

Gillian's daughter, Nicola, who at present it studying Aeronautical Engineering at Loughborough University has followed in her mothers and grandmothers footsteps becoming the third generation of Barratt lady coach drivers. She helps out driving coaches and running the office in her spare time and during University breaks.

Barratt's Coaches Ltd remains a family-owned business run by Gillian Barratt. The company relocated from Nantwich in 2006 and is now based in Millbuck Way, Sandbach. Currently concentrating on the British market rather than the continent, the firm's vehicles are certainly a far cry from the first elderly Dennis bought more than half a century ago. The present fleet, now mainly made up of Volvo coaches, have cost up to £230,000 each.

A fine memorial to business founder Walter Barratt.

Top left: A former Barratt's coach from the 1950s. **Left:** *Gillian Barratt.* **Top right:** *A Barratt's coach on a trip to the continent.* **Above:** *Gillian and mother Dorée.* **Below:** *Part of the Barratt's fleet.*

Speakman & Co. - Families in Law

Around 1926 Speakman & Hill became one of the largest law firms in Crewe when, following the death of a local solicitor Charles Henry Weaver, Roger Hill took over his practice. The firm continued trading as Speakman & Hill and moved to Charles Weaver's premises in Bank Chambers, Market Street, Crewe.

With the on-going regeneration of Crewe town centre during the 1930s Roger Hill decided to move the firm. In 1938 they moved to the current 180 Nantwich Road site, which was at the time largely residential.

Roger Hill took on his son Gerald Roger Hill and then Walter Neville Longden as Articled Clerks. Following their qualification they became partners and the firm was known as Speakman, Hill & Longden. During the 1970s another long-established practice, Garnett & Culey, was incorporated into the firm.

Some 150 years after the firm was first established by John Speakman, Laura Britton became the first female partner. Joining her father, David, the tradition of Speakman &. Co being a family-run business was restored. Today, the firm continues the custom established by Charles Speakman of giving an initial consultation free of charge, and now deals with property, wills and probate and family matters.

The firm of Speakman & Co. can be traced back over a hundred and fifty years to 1855 when John Speakman moved from Manchester to join Edward Delves Broughton in his practice in Hospital Street, Nantwich. By the early 1860s John Speakman's two sons were working for the firm: John Vaughn Speakman was an Articled Clerk and Charles Edward Speakman was a Solicitor's General Clerk. The firm subsequently moved to Welch Row, Nantwich. and opened an office in Crewe.

Following John Speakman's death, Charles Speakman qualified as a solicitor and became a partner in the firm. Charles Speakman remained in Crewe and held many public appointments including Clerk to the Magistrates Court and Registrar to the County Court. In 1890 he was joined by his niece's husband, Frank Flowerdew.

Following Frank Flowerdew's death in 1904, Charles Speakman practised on his own until 1910 when his nephew, Roger Wilbraham Hill, joined the firm which became known as Speakman & Hill.

Top left: Charles Edward Speakman. **Below:** Speakman & Co.'s 180 Nantwich Road, Crewe, premises.

Reaseheath College - A Growing Curriculum

Today Reaseheath College is the UK's leading land-based college. What was originally called the Cheshire School of Agriculture opened in 1921. The affiliated Worleston Dairy Institute had already been training girls in the ancient craft of cheese-making since 1892.

The number of students at the college in the 1920s was only around 60. Dairying was transferred to the main campus in 1926 when a women's hostel was built.

From the 1920s until the outbreak of the Second World War in 1939, the college provided one-year certificate courses in agriculture, poultry husbandry, dairying and horticulture.

By 1947 the number of courses available had expanded to include short courses in topics such as farmhouse cheese-making and a two year technical education course for the dairy industry. Outreach, day release and evening classes in agriculture and horticulture were also introduced.

Forty years later the college had grown in both size and diversity. There were now 265 full-time students and 1,425 part-timers, a staff of 130 and a budget of £2.4 million. Four out of ten full-time students studied farming courses.

In 1993 Reaseheath College was incorporated along with other colleges of further education by Act of Parliament, with its assets transferred from the Local Education Authority.

Reaseheath was the first land-based college in the country to have the distinction of receiving an 'Outstanding' Ofsted report, with top grades in every area. The college has been awarded Beacon College status, and was the first college in the North West to receive the Training Quality Standard in recognition of its excellent partnerships with industry.

A recent capital project of £20million has resulted in new buildings and educational facilities, including a specialist Learning Resource Centre and brand new Engineering Skills Academy. A further £12 million is being invested, including £4 million on phase two of the animal management centre and around £7 million to upgrade the Food Academy and Centre of Excellence.

Today's college is a dynamic, thriving enterprise. Student numbers have reached 900 full-time and 5,500 part timers in 17 programme areas. Staff numbers have risen to 300, and the annual budget to £9 million.

Top left: *Dairy students in the 1930s turning cheese as part of the cheesemaking process.* ***Above:*** *Girl's in the Women's Land Army in the Horticulture Department of Reaseheath College were trained in the techniques of market gardening.* ***Below:*** *Reaseheath College.*

ACKNOWLEDGMENTS

The publishers would like to sincerely thank a number of individuals and organisations for their help and contribution to this publication.

This book would have been almost impossible without the kind co-operation of the following:

Gordon Davies

Cheshire Archives & Local Studies Department

Nantwich Museum

Jim Carter

David Hey